sufficiently striking illustration of what we wish to convey, for we shall be met with the objection that, what may be easy in an infant may be impossible with an adult; that whereas, though the soft, tractable bone of a child may yield to pressure, the hard or brittle bone of the man may be unbending and intractable.

But it is not so; and we daily see malformations in persons who, from the nature of their business or occupation, become round-shouldered, bow-legged, and crooked-backed. We see the success with which curvature of the spine is treated, and wholly upon the principle that is followed in the use of the little machine before us.

But more to our purpose is the assertion, as stated by old historians, that the great Cyrus had a nose of peculiar shape, and that it became fashionable to have a nose such as his. This was accomplished by bandaging the member; and by using means by which it was pressed for a given time daily, in a direction à la Cyrus.

"There is nothing new under the sun," and this nose-machine was successfully used as far back as the time of Cyrus, the Persian king. Indeed, it is merely a matter of degree, for in a child ten years of age any effect by the machine is obtained in four or five days, in a person of twenty years in eight or ten, while in an individual of forty a full effect would be produced in about three weeks, and with the advanced in years, the nose is altered in shape by pressure in time varying with their years.

The Chinese admire a broad nose, and they easily get it, and that by adopting a plan in principle the same as here recommended, namely, *that of frequent and gentle direction of growth*. These people, as well as the negroes and others, effect their object by the rudest appliances, and they are successful to the end they think beautiful; but the little contrivance we are recommending is made upon scientific principles, effecting its object in so short a time and with so little inconvenience as probably would make an inhabitant of the Celestial Empire wonder greatly.

It often surprises us that medical men do not suggest to their patients whose features are plain in appearance that they have the cartilage of the centre of the face submitted to easy pressure, either right or left, up or or down, as circumstances require.

The bone of the human frame is very accommodating as to its taking different shapes, as well as in its healing from fractures; and it may be frequently observed that when there is any undue continuous pressure upon the frontal bone, identations and somewhat lasting malformations are observable. Crooked fingers, perverted great-toes, and cramped small ones are all produced by a more or less continuous pressure on or about the parts affected. Now, if such effects are the result of pressure upon bone, how much greater must be its action upon cartilage? If the hard bone of the head and the large lumbar of the spine can be directed differently to what is their normal state, the more likely it is that the nose, made of soft, tractable cartilage, should take a shape almost any pressure would give it.

More than one instrument has been constructed for the proper formation of the nose, with more or less success. The principal thing in these contrivances, of course, must be to be able to adjust the instrument in such a way as to give pressure in certain parts, but in these parts only. For instance, if the nose be thin at the point and large at the base, the pressure must not be at the tip, but at the base of the nose. And the difficulty has been in so contriving an instrument that it might be set to any guage, and kept at that until the object for which it has been used is obtained. This difficulty is now overcome, and we are making neat instruments that can be used without a disagreeable pressure, and that will effect the object aimed at in a remarkably short time. An hour during the day or night is sufficient for the wearing of these appliances. They can be sent to any part of the world by post, and the cost of them is not high, considering the important improvement they produce.*

In sending these contrivances for the improvement of the shape of the nose, the writer gives the fullest instructions for their use, and throws out some hints as to the shape desirable for good appearance, and gives replies to any question in connection with the subject. Diagrams of the nose have been forwarded to him, that he might inform country patients as to the best means to be used. This is certainly a great assistance in the affair, and nothing more is required for the purpose of choosing a machine suited to the case. Another plan is, though we do not recommend it, on account of trouble, to model the nose in any soft substance, such as wax, plaster, or gutta-percha, and forward the same to the seller of these instruments, who adjusts them accordingly. It is not an uncommon occurrence to find a crooked nose made straight for a time by the use of our machine for less than an hour. It is not a long time back that we first put one of these instruments on a crooked nose, and we held the patient in conversation while the machine retained his nose a prisoner. After a time the instrument was removed, and to the delight of the patient, his nose was straight and his face vastly improved. Of course, this change could hardly be expected to continue very long, unless it should be followed up by a few repetitions of the pressure, but it proved enough to show the patient that he had only to continue the use of the machine for a few days, when his nose would be an ornament to his face, rather than what it had been, a disfigurement.

We have a letter before us at this time from a lady who certainly has not used the instrument more than seven days, who says that in that time a "wonderful improvement has been made in the shape of the nose." Again, an ugly nose had a machine upon it; it was worn in a desultory way over a few weeks, and it is now as perfect a nose as you will see in a day's walk, or even ride; but it is of little use multiplying instances, and testimonials we eschew, as our patients neither like the trouble of being applied to, nor would they give their consent to our making use of their names. And this is as it should be; we charge for our instruments, and that is enough.

By taking a cast from a model, the owner would have a fuller opportunity of seeing the shape of this member, as he might turn it in any direction he pleased, and in fact, see the form of his nose as other people see it. We hope to say more about the nose at the end of this paper, and to handle it in a different manner, and to treat it to a different dressing to what we have just submitted it. And when we have done so, we believe that it will be none the worse for the treatment; on the contrary, if its form is not improved, the way for its amendment will be

---

* Unless a more complicated machine is required than is usually the case, the cost of the machine is 10s. 6d. Mr. A. Ross is anxious to give any other particulars respecting the machine, and therefore invites correspondence upon the subject

ade known, and there will be less excuse for it being poked here and there, when it may rather present itself, and that with grace and elegance; and instead of its being considered a nuisance, it may be an ornament; instead of being merely a mass of gristle, it may be a beautiful feature, holding the proud position of the centre of the human face, and thus being rendered conspicuous, to the admiration of all.

CHAPTER II.

Our last chapter upon Noses produced a great amount of interest, for it appeared as a magazine article, and we have been horrified with the descriptions, written and verbal, given by many persons of their prominent organ; we have also been interested in finding how great is the desire on the part of owners of badly-shaped noses for an improvemet by any reasonable means. And further, the commendations received in reference to the plan suggested for making an ill-shaped nose presentable are fully appreciated.

But since the appearance of this magazine article, we have had again and again practical illustrations of the successful working of the Nose Machine, and we can vouch for the accuracy of the assertion that there need not be one ugly nose in existence. We beg to be understood, wherever there is the substance to act upon, wherever there is cartilage, gristle, or hard flesh, the machine will guide it, direct it to a shape that shall be pleasing and profitable.

Several persons have applied to us without these requirements, and we regret to say have seemed disappointed that we could not assist them. We indeed have been pained when we have seen their disappointment, and wished that we could render them service, but their case was beyond our power. Where there is no nose, where from accident the member is entirely gone, our invention is useless, and therefore, to save regret to our friends and pain to ourselves, we would intimate that when the nose has decreased in size, from disease or accident, we can only suggest that other appliances be resorted to that have met with much praise, but which require a lengthened and even painful treatment. In our wish to serve our day and generation, we may remark here, that on such persons applying to us, we recommend them to competent surgeons, and to those skilled in the kind of work required.

It is not always that a well-formed nose is good in appearance, for although its symmetery may be perfect, there may be drawbacks so great that it may be most repulsive to look at. It will now be our object to describe these imperfections, and to prescribe for their amelioration.

Hair growing in the nostrils, from moles, and from the ears, is a sign of time, and proves that years of maturity, at least, are approaching. With an individual under twenty-five there is seldom found hair in the ears or nostrils. The hair grows wonderfully fast on these parts, and resembles in its appearance, &c., fungi in the vegetable world. Hair in the nostrils is produced in twenty-four hours, and it has been found that, under favourable circumstances, it has reproduced itself in a considerably less time than that. Under the microscope, these hairs appear different in shape to those of the head, and the naked eye can detect them as being of a more succulent character. A magnifying-glass

shows them to be perfectly flat, while those of the head are round, and cane-like in look. As no face with these hairs has a pleasing appearance, the following plan is recommended for their removal. A piece of wool, to which is attached a piece of thread, is put far into the nostril, with the thread hanging over the lips. A depilatory is then put up the nose, and allowed to remain there for a few minutes, during which time the root of the hair is in all probability destroyed. In cases where the root is unusually strong it is only impaired, and a second or even a third application must be resorted to. By this means the inside of the nose assumes its normal appearance, having that clear, red interior, so different to its appearance when these unsightly, dirty-looking hairs are growing with such profuseness. Some persons unwisely remove the hairs by forcibly extracting them. The tweezers and the thumb and finger are dexterously used. The pain produced in thus removing hair from the nostrils is not small, and the danger engendered is certainly great. Polypus and other diseases of the nose are often created by such treatment, and the irritation produced by plucking the hair always more or less causes swelling, and thus produces more disfigurement than the hair itself. It is a popular error to suppose that the depilatory affects the skin. This supposition doubtless has arisen from statements, made in large-circulating journals, the proprietors of which give recipes for the removal of superfluous hair, but emphatically impress upon their readers that they must be prepared to have the skin affected.

Another contingency to which the nose is subject is what the medical profession term *bacchia*. This disease commences by throwing up mounds of red skin, and it may be for many months that it takes no other form. Then may be perceived a chain of burrows extending to a second mound. This process continues till the nose becomes most unsightly. For the cure of this disease the greatest care is required in diet. Physical exercise is recommended, and mental rest. In some cases a more generous diet is suggested, but mostly less wine than spirits; a discontinuance of malt liquors and rich food is recommended. Aperient remedies are always prescribed in this case, and often an outward application of the following mixture :—Rose-water, 4 oz.; sulphate of zinc, 5 grains. Another is, almond oil, ½ oz.; liquid potass, 3 drops, a little rose-water or distilled water, shaken together. Sulphate of copper, 10 grains, in 8 oz. of rose-water, is good. This is somewhat a difficult complaint to prescribe for, until the person afflicted can give some particulars of his general health; and therefore, should any correspondence be required upon this particular deformity, it will be necessary to state age, mode of living, and occupation: if a personal interview cannot be arranged, a photograph would greatly assist in giving a knowledge of what is required. Polypus is a sad disease of the nose, and is frequently produced by violence, such as striking the nose, attempting to remove pimples by mechanical means, and by placing powerful pungent matters into close proximity to it. When polypus has formed, it is a matter for the treatment of a surgeon, and therefore quite useless for us to tender information, more than to strongly recommend that the individual so afflicted should not lose an hour in seeking surgical aid.

What is vulgarly called a flesh-worm is frequently found in the skin of the face, and most often in the exterior skin of the nose. These parasites show themselves in little black spots, producing a prickling, burning sensation. They are sometimes removed by pinching the skin, and thus forcing them from their occupation. A much better plan is to cauterise them, by which means they are killed (we speak advisedly, for they have life, which under the microscope is apparent). The writer provides patients in a case of this kind with a small bottle of liquid, which by the aid of a camel-hair brush is carefully applied to the little black spots. After one or two usings of this article the creature loses life, and then, by applying a little cold cream and a towel, it comes from its imbedded place with the greatest facility. As the indentations made by these worms are small, the skin, from its elasticity, fills up the small punctures after the removal of the worm, and the nose assumes all its former appearance. The liquid used for destroying these objectionable specks does not discolour the skin, as might be expected, for when we speak of cauterising we generally associate blackness with the operation. It is therefore pleasing to be able to say that with the use of this liquid no discolouration whatever is produced. Freckles of the nose are another disfigurement to which it is subject, and when these become widespread upon its surface, the same liquid as we have just mentioned is used. By its use the freckle is decomposed, and Nature, in recovering herself, produces skin of a better colour. A few freckles of not a large kind appearing upon the nose may be cured by Ross's Skin Tonic, which is an astringent liquid used in many cases for imperfections of the skin. This liquid is applied to a nose soft and uneven in surface, as it gives hardness, from its astringent qualities.

The nose in many cases would be greatly improved if the skin over and around it were of a less loose kind—if its covering could be drawn tighter and kept firm by the skin in its neighbourhood being less yielding. Some persons may have the skin of the nose of uniform thickness, proper elasticity, and of a firm texture; but from the skin of the face being generally of a flabby tendency, the appearance of this feature is entirely marred. As a remedy, a liquid is generally used that contracts the skin. From time immemorial the gums have been washed with tooth-water for tightening the teeth, which, as a rule, has the effect of preventing the falling-out of the incisor teeth; and which had it not been used, the sacrifice would certainly not have been small. It is upon this plan that a liquid is used to the skin of the nose, in order to tighten its texture, and to act healthily upon the *epidermis*. Six or seven applications of this astringent have a marked effect, and looseness or flabbiness of the skin is greatly reduced in a few days by the application of this liquid. In cases where the nose is unhandsomely large, this astringent preparation is most useful. The large panniers seen on some noses take often proper proportions after using the shrinker. Even slight marks from small-pox disappear, and indentations are levelled up in a surprising manner.

CHAPTER III.

As we have shown in our previous chapters, the desire to improve the shape of the nose is not small. Doubtless this arises from the fact that it is a great distinguishing mark of character, both moral and intellectual. Intelligent persons do not always have a nose beautiful in form, but it is always of a character that is significant. The great Napoleon was greatly in favour of a large nose. He used to remark, "Give me a man with a good allowance of nose. When I want any head-work done, I choose a man with a long nose, and providing he is an educated man, it is better done by him than by another." Napoleon further remarked that he generally found a long nose and a long head go together. It does not require much observation to find that most of the individuals of marked intellect, of energetic character, of moral power, and of genius, have, as a rule, large noses. If you notice the men of mark in France, you will see this; so among Englishmen, and with the Italians. Take, as a proof that large noses are indicative of talent, the foremost men of Europe—those men who have risen to their high position by their energy and superiority. Commence with Napoleon, and finish with Bismarck, and you will find that, without exception, character is shown in a marked manner in the size of the nose. It is true that Socrates had a small nose in comparison with his wonderfully large head and face, but the shape of his nose was most significant, and under ordinary circumstances perhaps it might have been considered an average-sized feature, although small by comparison. Of so great importance is the shape of the nose to the forehead, that it may, as Lavater expresses it, be considered the abutment to the brain. We cannot conceive of an intelligent-looking forehead without a well and full-sized nose. If the abutment be not sufficiently substantial, and of nobleness of appearance, the superstructure will be insignificant. Indeed, the nose as a point from which the quality of the forehead is judged, and the upper part of the head receding from the nose, or overhanging it, produces a difference in the estimate of the character of no small degree. Few countenances can be considered ugly when the nose is of proper size and good shape; it is a regulator of nearly all the other parts of the face. A nose of proportionate length and breadth will make the mouth of pleasing appearance, will give good contour to the cheeks and chin, and will improve the look of every part of the face but the eyes; and even these, some might contend, are improved by the influence which a well-formed nose has upon the forehead in which they are set. Some of the comments in the newspapers upon the Nose Machine have led the public to suppose that persons can have any kind of nose they please by using the machine. This is not quite correct, and if an individual with a small Grecian nose is desirous of having a large Aquiline member, he will be disappointed in our instrument. The *Echo* of the 9th November, adverting to our machine, says that for 10s. 6d. you may shape the nose as you please, and the *Sunday Times* says there will be a fashion in noses; but we say, if that fashion should happen to be of a large tendency, as with chignons and hoop-petticoats, and other details of fashion of late, there may be much difficulty in keeping up to the standard quantity, for this our machine does not supply, but confines its operations to shape, to form, and beauty.

There have been instances where accidents have occurred by which an individual has been deprived of this useful member, and a substitute has been supplied by a piece of silver the shape of a nose; the skin of the forehead has been peeled down, and the metallic nostril thus covered. This skin has joined the greater body of flesh near the lips and cheek-bones, and the whole has thus become a perfect contrivance both as to usefulness and appearance. In some such instances the patient has been far from prepossessing when the original nose existed, but under the surgeon's hands he has been both mended and *decorated*.

The nose should be exactly of the same length as the forehead. There should be a slight indentation at the top of the nose. Looking at it full in front, the back, *dorsum, spina nasi*, should be decidedly broad. The end of the nose, *orbiculus*, must be neither hard nor fleshy. This point of the nose is often termed the *button*. The outline of this part should, to be handsome, be most definite. It should not finish off with a point, neither should it end with a nob of undue thickness. The *pinnæ*, or sides of the nose, must be properly defined. Viewed sideways, the lower part of the nose should be about one-third its whole length. The upper part of the nostrils should be pointed, and below they should be perfectly round; they should be divided into equal parts by the profile of the lip. Lavater says, " The sides of the nose, or its arch, should be like a wall. Above it must close well with the arch of the eyebone, and the eye must be at least half an inch in breadth." This is the shape our contrivance, in the character of a machine, tends to form; and we can assert, without fear of contradiction, that our advice having been followed, not a few noses have altered for the better their appearance.

Physiognomically, a nose that has small nostrils generally belongs to persons of little enterprise or spirit. The open-breathing nostril is indicative of sensibility. It is remarked the Dutch nose is considered a bad nose. The Italians have good noses, and the English not bad ones. The Tartars have flat, indented noses, the negroes have broad noses, and the Jews have *hawk* ones. The nose that is narrow near the forehead shows power of mind, but power that is impulsive, and not of endurance. Our Swift, as also, according to our pictures, Cæsar Borgia, Titian, and Paul Sarpi, had what is called the broad-backed nose. Such is not met with in one person in ten thousand, and when seen it may be depended upon as belonging to a man of intellectual superiority.

The commanding nose, as it is called, is one that is arched at the upper part, and it may be found to belong to all persons who successfully carry out any exploit that depends mainly upon the direction of great forces. Such a nose had Wellington, and, more or less, it is delineated in the portraits of most if not all the successful warriors, ancient and modern.

The Grecian nose is most beautiful for women, and it is rarely that a painter ventures to give his heroine any other. The novelists, in their description of their favourite lady, seldom omit to describe her with such a feature. The poets write many lines on this member of beauty, and the lover, " if he write woful ballads to his mistress's eyebrow," thinks as much of her nose. The sculptor puts much work into this feature, knowing full well that it influences for good all the other parts of the human face. Even the photographer will place his visitor in such a position previously to taking the *carte-de-visite* as shall cover by shade the ugly part of the nose, or light up with " high light " that part worthy of prominence. Expression in the nose seems absurd, but Byron says :—

> " In his eye
> And nostril beautiful disdain, and might,
> And majesty flash their full lightnings by,
> Developing in that one glance the Deity."

The inducement is great to repeat the many interesting things said by poets and writers, both old nad modern, about this feature; but we are reminded of want of space, and the calls upon us for subject-matter under other heads on this important subject, the Nose.* So we will leave this portion of our subject alone for a while, and conclude our brief chapter by remarking that nothing is much easier than taking a model and cast of the nose with plaster of Paris; and it serves the purpose well for adjusting the Nose Machine, as do pictures and drawings with which some of our patrons have favoured us.

While writing this article, we have had brought to our notice quite a striking illustration of what we have asserted above, that the beauty of the countenance greatly depends upon the nose. The case we refer to is that of a young lady of sixteen years of age, of good complexion, good eyes, and pleasing expression; but her nose is bad in shape, and covered with indentations from small-pox. The other parts of the face are free from marks, and the virulence of the disease has shown itself upon this prominent feature only, and has left its marks to such an extent as to mar the whole beauty of the face. The remedy, of course, is the filling-up of the indentations with an elastic pigment, and thus to hide the marks left by that fell disease, small-pox. And as the outline of this feature is broken by the marks only, it is quickly, though superficially, remedied by the pigment.

Such an alteration is thus made, that whereas such a person was almost repulsive to behold on account of the appearance of the nose, in its natural condition—indeed, sickening to look at—by covering over the unsightly parts, you see a countenance not only pleasurable, but even handsome. Such contrasts as these establish us more and more in our belief that the beauty of the face depends greatly upon the shape and elegance of this central feature; and that when it is at fault, the Nose Machine is its remedy.

CHAPTER IV

There are some remarkable practices and uses to which the nose is put; amongst them is that of administering narcotics, as being the most expeditious means of affecting the brain. Excessive smoking will act upon the stomach, and through the latter upon the brain; but, if the fumes of tobacco are driven through the nostrils, the brain is more thoroughly and quickly acted upon. So with opium and all narcotics. In the East smokers puff the fumes of opium from the back of the mouth through the nose, and by thus doing find both expedition and economy in their transition from a world of reality to a state of short but ecstatic bliss.

"The divine weed," as Byron called it, is kept in the mouth by some, and after being acted upon by the saliva, it begins slowly to affect the head through the stomach; but when sniffed up the nose in the form of snuff, immediate action upon the nerves is obtained. It is believed that the negro often plugs the nose with moistened tobacco, that a fuller and more decided result may be produced than would otherwise be the case if he used the narcotic as is generally done. This negro is a nasty fellow; and so eager does he become for the stimulant of tobacco-juice,

---

* This is in reference to the many deaths connected with a wide-circulating magazine, the articles of which treat upon all matters connected with good looks. It can be had through all booksellers, direct from the Editor Alex. Ross,

that he will swallow it with avidity, and will even masticate and put into his stomach the herb itself.

The practice of sniffing, pulling, rubbing, and picking the nose seems to have originated from the monkey tribe, and, is simply disgusting, and is a sure indication of bad-breeding. Necessity compels the use of a kerchief, but it should be seen as little as possible, and never at those times when much company is present, or at meal-times. We have seen beautiful ladies, whom to see was to admire, who when at ease, or when meditative, had the horrid habit of unduly handling or fingering their noses. The practice is so revolting, that it requires to be seen but once performed to produce the very opposite of admiration in a person of any sensibility.

Some men in conversation can only continue lengthened speeches by vigorous picking of the nose, but however, useful their remarks or lucid their description, the hearer loses, through the disgust created by the action much of their value, and is glad to be a good three feet from the ill-bred creatures. It is bad enough to see a man or woman put dark and dirty pungent dust up the nose, but to be present at its removal or the cleaning-out of a nose, however good in shape, is only a fit position for a dustman. This habit of picking the nose is sometimes witnessed in public speakers, and if any given to such tricks, should read these remarks, we beg to assure them that whatever their oratorical powers may be, they will never command the ear, the respect, or the applause of their audience while they practise this worst of all bad habits.

There are many instances on record of total separations of friends through such bad habits as these. George the Fourth, a perfect gentleman in manners, formed many serious dislikes to some near and dear to him through such simple but disgusting doings. Divorces and judicial separations often may be traced to similar things as first causes, and lasting bad impressions often accrue by them, when otherwise sweet and continued friendship would exist.

In a previous chapter upon this subject, we spoke of the flesh-worm so frequently met with in the skin of the fair nose, and sometimes in that of the dark one. This disease produces a great deal of itching, causing the patient to rub and scratch the nose, and thus cause him to acquire a habit against which we have been disclaiming. A little glycerine will allay the irritation for a time, or even a little sweet oil will give ease; but as an effectual cure, nothing will succeed so well as passing the caustic liquid carefully over them by the aid of a small brush, so as to entirely eradicate them by cauterisation, as before suggested.* Hair growing in the nostrils is another inducement to form a habit which, when thoroughly acquired, becomes most difficult to overcome, but which, if persisted in, lowers one from a well-bred person, it may be, to at least an undesirable individual.

The appearance of the nose is greatly altered by the habits practised—either good or bad. This is not peculiar to the nose, for by discipline and good tuition, the mouth, chin, and the general countenance are greatly and quickly improved. In cases of lawlessness and dissipation, the nose undergoes a rapid change, and the indulgence of any intemperance produces upon it a transformation perfectly marvellous. The great physiognomist,

---

* This liquid the writer supplies at the cost of 8s. 6d. per bottle, or it will be sent by post upon the receipt of the amount in stamps.

Lavater tells a striking anecdote in illustration of this. He said that a young and innocent girl, who had been educated in the country, and had been kept from all guile and evil companionship, found herself with candle in hand before the looking-glass in her sleeping-room. With extreme modesty and commendable humility she quickly withdrew, fearing the intrusion of pride and vanity. In a few days' time she was invited to pay a visit to some London friends. She spent many weeks among gay scenes and many admirers. The flattery received from companions, and the bad influences engendered from vanity, gaiety, and thoughtlessness, told upon this young lady too quickly, and in a few months produced a vast influence upon her character. Having paid her London visit, she returned to her quiet country home, and one evening found herself, light in hand, before her mirror. Now she could bear to look at its reflection. Her heart was less sensitive to evil, and vanity and pride had induced her many times to gaze upon her reflection without a desire for humility. As she looked, she became sad at the contrast that existed between her appearance now and what it had been. The open, truthful, becoming look of innocence had gone, and had made room for the bold and haughty look of Vanity Fair. Her sadness became sorrow, and her grief almost despair, when she thought of how great a good she had lost,—a beautiful face and innocent soul. I do not recollect whether the narrator informs his readers that the lady ever recovered her looks, or purity of soul and mind; but this much is sufficient to illustrate the fact that we all, more or less, have it in our power to improve our looks by paying attention to our characters, by giving heed to discipline, tuition, and every good quality.

Anecdotes, judging from the largeness of their number, are generally enjoyed, particularly when they are told well, and are not prosy; therefore, although the temptation is great to write something about the custom of rubbing noses as a mode of salutation, and of the ornamental custom of wearing rings through the nostrils, and a hundred other things in connection with the nose, we will complete this chapter with the relation of a few anecdotes and wise sayings, as little prosy as possible, and told as briefly and as succinctly as possible.

An anxious father was once asked by his son, who was about leaving home for a distant town, what he should bring on his return to his parent. "You have been very good to me, father, and when I have made my way in yon city, I will bring you something to endeavour to compensate you for your self-denial. Say, what shall it be?" "Ah! my dear boy," replied the father, "I shall be more than content if you will return with the *countenance* you now have. Let me see indexed on your face goodness and truth. I want no more."

Lavater says a hundred flat noses may be met with in men of great prudence, discretion, and abilities of various kinds; but when the nose is very small, and has an inappropriate upper lip, or when it exceeds a certain degree of flatness, no other feature or lineament of the countenance can rectify it.

Noses without any remarkable character, without gradation, without curvature, without undulation, without any designable delineation, may indeed be found with rational, good, and occasionally, in some degree, superior characters, but never with such as are truly great and excellent.

A nose which easily and continually turns up in wrinkles is seldom to be found in truly good men; so those which will scarcely wrinkle, even

with an effort, are seldom seen in men consummately wicked. When noses
which not only easily wrinkle, but have traces of their wrinkles indented
in them, are found in good men, these good, well-disposed men are half
fools.

CHAPTER V.

With a certain amount of truth, it is said that mediocrity is imposed upon
by the learned, that the scientific impose upon the credulity of the un-
itiated, and that the vulgar are led in their belief according to the whim
of learned bodies. The world is now becoming too old for philosophers to
have it so much their own way as formerly, and the contradictions as to
the sun going round the world, and the wrong calculations in merely a
million or so of miles as to the distance of the sun from the earth, with
disagreements upon matters of theology, chemistry, geology, and almost
all the sciences, have led the public to be more exacting for proof of any
statement in connection with science. Indeed a portion of the public are
exceedingly incredulous, and often refuse to believe in those doctrines which
may fairly be presumed to be correct. Physiognomy is one of the sciences
which a number of people question, and although accepted by many to be
true, an incredulous few refuse to accept. To an observant person this seems
strange, for the facility of testing the truth of the laws of this science is
great, and every man's face is presumed to be an index by which, by comparison, his character can be guessed at.

In order to give the incredulous the opportunity of comparing their own
characters, morally and intellectually, with the statement made by the
believers in the science of physiognomy, we purpose giving the rules for
judging character by one feature, and that feature the most indicative of
any—namely, the nose. Let the inquirer, without prejudice, fully study
this part of physiognomy, and then proceed to investigate the subject in
connection with the other features, and we believe he will be a true
disciple of Lavater.

> "Man only has the face erect, the nose,
> The mouth minute, the eye with acute angle."

Persons with rudely-rounded noses are found to be harsh in character,
and so in more or less degree are they who possess very sharp or small
noses. A concave root of the nose is not elegant, yet the person to whom it
belongs is an attractive person, and is generally beloved.

The despotic man may be recognised by the under-lip projecting and
the nose turned up. This nose has facetiously been called the celestial
one, but only, we presume, on account of its turning towards the heavens,
and it is of all noses earthly and tyrannical. Nero had such a nose and
such a character. Tyranny has a great influence upon the shape of this
feature. The Peruvians are an exemplification of this, as it is known that
the nose of that people has undergone a great deterioration since the
Spaniards had the control over their destinies.

Arched and pointed noses show tact. The blunt nose indicates an
absence of this faculty. Vesalius had a fine characteristic nose, and

a good portrait of him would greatly assist in showing what a resemblance
exists between a Vesalius-shaped nose and nobleness of character and
soundness of mind.   When the tip of the nose is hard and firm, it shows a
love of ease, and an inclination to engage only in those undertakings that
are easily accomplished.   Creative power—the inventive genius—is seen
more in the eye and forehead than elsewhere; but the nose of such has
its peculiarity, which may be seen in Watt, Brunel, and in the faces of
such inventive, imaginative persons as Dickens, Thackeray, and Collins.
Dean Swift and Cervantes' portraits will show the mark.   The nose of
Cicero is a perfect study of penetrating acuteness and power of discernment.   The following remarkable characters, whose portraits can be obtained without difficulty, have noses which are great indices of what were
their great characteristics while the originals lived:—Charles I., Julius
Cæsar, the Fredericks of Prussia, Hogarth, Rembrandt.   A more perfect
idea of the shape of the nose in connection with character may be obtained
by the study of plaster busts of Milton, Locke, Shakespeare, Bunyan, and
Napoleon.   The portrait of Voltaire has a nose showing power of thought
and keen sensibility in its owner.   An examination of such a nose as this
will establish the fact in the inquirer's mind that as is the shape of the
nose so is the character of the individual to whom it belongs.   At this
moment we have before us the portrait of a notorious fool, celebrated for
his connection with and the notice he obtained for his unwise doings.   Before us also are the portraits of the wise, the good, and the learned, and the
contrast in the appearance of the noses of the former with those of the latter
is most discernible, and it is not difficult to detect the gradation from the nose
of the clever person to those of the persons of ability and genius, and even
the gradation in the range of genius from great to greater.   The power of
observation is greater in some individuals than in others, and those of
small power in this particular who are anxious to tell character by the
nose we beg to compare this feature in opposite known persons, as in
Howard and Bonaparte, Voltaire and Bunyan, Newton and Nelson, and a
thousand others who readily present themselves to the mind of the reader.
By this practice the student will soon become proficient in discerning by
the size, shape, and colour of the nose what is in the heart and mind of man.
This being only a part of physiognomy, the knowledge will be less complete than if the whole of the science were studied; but this part of the
face is certainly fuller of indications than any other; and whereas a complete knowledge of physiognomy would require several months of observation, this part of the subject, with all its bearings, could be acquired in as
many days.   Hence, as far as good appearance is concerned, the importance
of our invention.

CHAPTER III.

Surely it will be allowed, by all who have given attention to the subject, that there exists harmony between moral and corporeal beauty.
It is rare indeed to find a man of intellectual beauty, apart from a face
interesting at least to look upon, and more often with an eye of brilliant
expression, a mouth indicative of sentiment, and a nose beautiful in
form or conspicuous for size and proportion.   If it be true—and who
can doubt it?—that there is a similarity in physical and moral develop-

ment, then may a mans character be easily told by the size and shape
of his features. It is not the case that, by improving the shape of the features,
which many do by contrivance, the character undergoes any change. And it
should be understood that the face, in its natural condition, is the only one
from which character should be judged. Doubtless those whose tendencies,
intellectually and morally, are in the wrong direction, may delude the be-
holder, by adopting measures for altering the appearance of the eye, and
covering with hair an indifferent part of the chin or forehead. Although
this is done with a desire to hide that which they consider objectionable,
and therefore meets somewhat with our approbation on that account, yet we
would recommend that a cultivation of the mind and an improvement of
character be attended to, for the thorough alteration of the features. It is
believed that a cultivation of oratory improves the shape and beauty of the
mouth, as gluttony intensifies any ugliness it may possess. A linguist has,
as a rule, a good eye, and persons not handsome in this particular may prove
it by acquiring a knowledge of languages. Music, attempting a recollection
of localities and individuals, as well as the cultivation of ideality, imitation,
order, colour, and number, will alter for the better the shape of the upper
part of the face. The cultivation of benevolence, veneration, hope, and con-
scientiousness will give an improved aspect to the face. It is not difficult
to account, either phrenologically or otherwise, for the great degeneration
in the formation and healthiness of the nose in persons addicted to evil
ways, but it is quite certain that no feature undergoes such a change for
the worse when evil habits are indulged in as does the nose. Secretiveness
will shrink it. Intemperance will make it blotchy and uneven, fill it with
pimples and specks, and alter its contour greatly.

Pride and vanity will give it an ugly turn in the wrong direction.
Self-esteem and contempt for others will give a further move in that
direction, which will at once put it far beyond anything handsome to
behold. Excessive care, or extravagant anxiety, a craving for abundance,
covetousness, malice, and every evil poor humanity is prone to, immediately
tell upon this feature in particular; although every other, much or little,
partakes of disadvantages from the same causes. As we have said in a
former chapter, Lavater depended more upon the nose for information
regarding character than he did upon any other part of the face, and he was
right; for it is most sensitive to the effects of evil and good, and readily
indicates the state of mind, soul, and heart of its owner. We have heard
a hairdresser say, that from his continually handling the hair, he could tell
the state of the health of any individual from the peculiarity of its texture,
dryness, and other phenomena; and we have little doubt but that, at a
glance at the nose, any physiognomist could tell the health of an individual,
in body and in mind.

As to appearance, the nose is the most important part of the face. If it
be not of good form, no other constituent in the countenance will make up
for it. Here is a negative proof of its consequence; the poets of all nations
have sung in praise of the eyes, the mouth, the chin, and even the hair,
but hardly a line has been written leading one to a pleasant contemplation
of this much-abused feature. Humorists have pulled pretty lustily at the
nose, and wrung many a peal of fun from its peculiarities. If a countenance is, then, to be pleasing in appearance, and if it is within the range of
possibility to make the nose good in shape, let no means be left unemployed
to this desirable end.

AN ESSAY

UPON

THE HUMAN HAIR,

AND

ITS REPRODUCTION BY THE STIMULANT SPANISH FLY, OR CANTHARIDES.

PRICE ONE PENNY.

———◆———

BY ALEX: ROSS,

Inventor of the Hair Dye, Depilatory, and other Hair Preparations.

———◆———

Many hundreds of individuals apply to the writer of this short essay, as to the means for recovering an ornament which is prized, more or less, by us all. The pleasure of describing what the hair is, and how it should be treated, was at first pleasant, but after years of repetition it became irksome in the extreme. And this small pamphlet was written to enlighten the public, and save labour to the writer. Not only so, but these pages will show why that great remedy, Spanish Fly Oil so signally succeeds in most cases of imperfect hair.

So difficult is it to give verbally a lengthened statement of the advantages arising from the use of Cantharides Oil for the growth of hair, that it becomes necessary to adopt a written medium for that purpose; also the difficulty is produced, not from a want of an accumulation of facts, but through oral explanations reaching but the few, and not, like an essay, finding its way to hundreds and thousands of persons suffering from thinness of hair, or disadvantaged in their appearance by meagre locks.

Hair may be thought by some to be a subject too trivial to engage the attention of the studious. If an excuse or a reason be required for this study by those so engaged, they may show that their subject has been the theme of the poet and the labour of the painter; that its antiquity is attractive, for the Assyrians, Egyptians, ancient Jews, as well as the people of more classical days, prided themselves in the arranging, beautifying, and promoting the growth of an auxiliary to beauty surpassed by none in its charms. The individual devoting the energies of a life to this subject, may remark to those who depreciate his engagement, that the wonders contained within its limits are more than enough for the contemplation of many lives; and like the manipulator with an atom or a globule of water, or the chemist with an examination into the laws of caloric, and the electrician inquiring into the wonders of electricity, he finds that nothing in nature is so insignificant as it at first appears, neither is there anything so small but what is more than sufficient to feed with mental food the mind of man. This is strikingly so with the subject of hair; and it is hoped before the reader completes the reading of this brief essay, that his opinion will be the same as the writer's.

A deficiency of the natural covering called hair, produces often disease and death. It is not only true that the bear and wild dog in the arctic regions could not long exist without its protection, but it is equally a fact that man when prematurely bald, or suddenly deprived of hair, is most susceptible to catarrh. So well known is this, that the greater number perhaps of persons wearing perukes do so more as a protection against cold than for the sake of ornament. The chest containing the vital organs, induces persons very wisely to protect that part of the body with scrupulous care; but should the chest be kept uncovered, nature, ever beneficent, causes hair to grow upon the neglected part in sufficient quantities, showing, in so doing, the importance not only of keeping that part of the body covered, but that hair is a great preventive to inflammation, other diseases, and death. Plants are provided with this covering, that the sun's rays may not be too powerful for them, or that the piercing winds may not do them injury. It is true that these filaments—found upon all plants except those that grow under water—collect from a humid atmosphere the moisture necessary to their well-being; but important as this office is in the existence of vegetation, it is perhaps subordinate to that of protection from excessive heat or cold.

As an ornament, nothing surpasses well-arranged hair, and its suitable decoration principally depends upon its profusion, obtained only through care and cultivation. The painter does not consider his Beauty perfectly charming unless her locks flow plentifully in brightness and thickness—the colour beautiful, and the gloss rich and radiant. The poet will "write a woful ballad to (so small a portion of hair as) his mistress' eyebrow," the inference being that if a few hairs upon the face inspire him with admiration and love, to how much greater an extent of rapture or enthusiasm would he rise in contemplating her flowing locks, "dishevelled, but in wanton ringlets waved." And the sculptor is not forgetful of the effects produced by a judicious use of what the divine Milton calls "golden tresses." But if the poets be taken as guides as to the amount of attention and enthusiasm to be given to the hair, then we shall find that we are to admire it more than any other constituent part of beauty.

But let us give some few particulars of a scientific kind respecting that which men have admired from the earliest times till now. The learned Liebig has analyzed it, and informs us that it consists of hydrogen, oxygen, nitrogen, and sulphur. In the possession of the writer is the hair of nearly every class, genera, and family of the mammalia, and upon examination all are found to contain more or less of these component parts. In this interesting collection may be found the hair of the Hottentot, American, Sikh, Asiatic, African —hair belonging to an individual a hundred years old, and the beautiful silky covering for the head of the earliest infancy. Fair hair contains the most sulphur and oxygen; black the most hydrogen and carbon. The hair upon the face has less sulphur and more carbon than that of the head.

Every hair grows from a follicle, or sheath, which is below the skin. This sheath is not positioned perpendicularly, but obliquely, and at its base has a pouch containing the bulb of the hair. The bulb is pulpy and cone-shaped, and is apparently made up of minute blood-vessels. This bulb is coated with a reflection of the shield or follicle. The hair is secreted from the surface of this bulb, forming one layer after another, the earlier ones rising above the surface. Very naturally it will be asked, how is it that any one, even with the most powerful microscope and other able appliances, could examine the human skin and hair so fully as to be able to distinctly point out the workings of nature in this particular? It has been distinctly ascertained that the hair of a lion is formed in the same way as the hair of any other animal; and it is fairly believed that the fine hairs, such as that of the small animals, are secreted in a similar manner, so that the above description of the growth of hair in man is taken from analogous structures investigated in other creatures. The hair, when examined by the microscope, will be found not to be of a uniform shape; few are perfectly cylindrical, and some are even grooved, and almost three-sided. Curly hair is generally found to be flat; and the whisker and moustache are mostly of this shape. A negro's hair is perfectly flat, and each hair is considerably broader than it is thick, partaking under the magnifying glass of the shape of the common flag seen in the gardens round London.

It has been pretty generally believed that hair is hollow; but late examinations go to prove that it is solid. This is no doubt the case; and Weber, who is allowed to be an authority upon this subject, gives it as his opinion that such is the fact. No doubt the unequal refraction of the light led former investigators into the belief as to its being tubular. The diameter of the human hair varies considerably. The Maltese perhaps have the coarsest. The average diameter is said to be one-three hundredth and one-five hundredth part of an inch. The length attained depends upon health, predisposition, and cultivation. In the Exhibition of 1862 hair was exhibited of the immense length of seventy-two inches; the colour was light; or what is laconically called an English brown. It belonged to one of England's fair daughters. Change of colour, both with male and female, commences at the temples and the back of the ears. No doubt this effect is partly, if not altogether, produced by the alkali in soap used in washing coming in contact more particularly with those parts; and in further proof of this, we might mention the fact that the hair upon the face, although it does not make its appearance till twenty or twenty-five years after that of the hair upon the head, is the first to become grey. And if further proof be necessary, we would remark that for experiment, the colouring matter of the hair may be nearly altogether removed by immersing it for a considerable time in powerful potash and water. The general impression is that the darker the hair the stronger the animal. Veterinary surgeons assert that the black horse is stronger and healthier than the chesnut-coloured, and that a white animal is delicate, if not unhealthy. In the purchasing of horses, white legs are eschewed and dark ones preferred. Of course, there are many exceptions to this rule. It is well known that the Scotch are fair and light-haired, and yet are a sturdy, powerful race; and that the Danes are athletic, brave, and perhaps as long-lived as any people in Europe, and would compare favourably as to longevity with the dark-haired Italian.

The analogy that exists between hair and vegetation is most striking. The plant increases in height and bulk by stimulating the root; it becomes fully developed by the use of the exciting properties found in the many applications used by the farmer and nurseryman. So is it with the natural production provided for the covering of animals. If a stimulant be applied, it will be found to assume more lengthy and bulky appearances. Hair is acted upon with great rapidity by exciting compounds. When Cantharides Oil is used to the skin upon which hair is growing, it will immediately be seen to derive fresh life and vigour from the oil's vivifying properties. It is often found that after an illness the hair falls plentifully from the head. This is produced by a general relaxation of the skin, which is immediately obviated by the use of the Cantharides Oil. Like the thirsty plant imbibing the moisture given it, and instantly becoming stronger and more beautiful from the refreshing shower, so is the hair as quickly altered for the better by the use of a stimulant.

No doubt there are other preparations, when used with discretion, well-suited to produce health to this beautiful ornament; but it is allowed by all who have had an opportunity of judging, that Cantharides Oil, or oil prepared from that curious and interesting little insect the Spanish fly, is by far the best for the purpose.

The same analogy exists in the treatment of the hair by pruning or cutting. It is so self-evident that both plants and hair are improved by cutting at periodical times, that it is unnecessary to make any further remarks upon this head. In the *fall*, or at the end of the year, the hair, like vegetation, undergoes a change. The sap seems to have a less rapid circulation, or even to remain stagnant. It is said that more greyness is perceptible at this time than at any other, and that it is at the fall of the year that the first grey hair is discovered. In the spring, the lightness of shade will give place to a darker hue, and the hair, like its prototype, will assume as great a change for the better. The growth of an old tree bears a great contrast with the fructifying powers of one that is young, but not more so than is perceptible in that of old and young hairs.

The most remarkable similarity, however, is in the physiology of the hair. What is the doctrine as to the propagation of vegetation? It is that their kind is continued either by seeds or cuttings. It has been long known to some that hair may be transplanted or propagated from cuttings. Hitherto it has been impossible to do this to so great an extent as to be of any very useful purpose, more than to prove that the analogy between it and vegetation, in this particular, is quite perfect. It may be interesting to many to inform them how the experiment with the cutting of a hair may be made; and should they feel sufficient interest to make an attempt at propagation, they will find the task far less difficult than it would seem from the directions.

A hair that is fine in texture, and that is quite healthy, should be selected. It should then be put into the eye of a fine needle, and bent over as with a piece of ordinary cotton, but with sufficient care to prevent the hair snapping. A stitch should then be taken in the scarf-skin, being careful not to draw the blood. If the experimentist dip the needle below the upper or scarf-skin, he will fail in the experiment. The best part of the body for an exemplification is the fleshy part of the arm. Having taken the stitch, the hair should be drawn through the puncture till the thickest part of the hair, or that part where the disconnection was made, is hidden under the skin. The needle may then be taken away, and the hair left to make root, which it will do in the course of a few days. In order to protect the hair (we had almost written plant) while striking or taking root, it will be well to place a piece of soft linen rag over it winding the same once or twice round the arm. In the space of a fortnight, or less, the hair will be firmly fixed, and it would then be interesting to measure its length, continuing to do so at stated intervals. The hair is very elastic, and capable of being stretched one-third its length, so that to get at a knowledge of its progress it is well to measure with care.

The writer having from observation found that these similarities and interesting matters existed, based upon these facts remedies for the hair's diseases and deficiencies, which it is purposed to treat briefly as we proceed. As was hinted, our subject is full of wonder, and is more than sufficient to feed the mental curiosity of many minds. One other surprising doctrine promulgated is that there is a decided connection existing betwixt the loss of hair, its change of colour, and a phrenological development; that is to say, the organs in their growth affect the hair, in quantity or quality, so that if an individual have any of the phrenological organs unduly acted upon, the hair will suffer. Take as an illustration a man with an unusual amount of conceit—one whose organ of self-esteem is large, and which has been increased by the mere pampering to his failing; such a person will have the meagre, ugly baldness just at the crown of the head. And so with the person who is philanthropic to excess— who does actions great in charity, and by so doing deprives himself of that which nature and circumstance would justly permit him to have. His benevolence is overdone—not justifiable. He has forgotten, perhaps, that charity can be carried to an unjustifiable extent. Such an individual will have the fine open countenance peculiar to such; but how produced? By the organ of benevolence, situated over the forehead, becoming sparely covered, if not altogether deprived of hair. Then, again, the person given to poetry will probably have the high temple, or IDEALITY, uncovered. We would not wish to convey the idea that all persons so losing the natural covering of the head, or becoming grey, are in character such as we have described. The imperfections may be produced by disease of the hair, caused by ill-health of the body, or by appliances not suited to its healthiness. But what we assert is this, that if individuals unduly use certain organs, the hair immediately over them will suffer to some extent, either in quantity or quality.

These few pages are sadly deficient for the conveying to the public the many facts accumulated by the studious observer upon this subject. Had there been space, it might have been shown that, though the chemical analysis of the hair of the mammalia is nearly the same, yet in other respects it is so different, that it is surprising our leading naturalists do not make it more a mark of distinction than they do in the animal kingdom. Linnæus and Cuvier, in their arrangement of the mammalia into families, orders, and genera, might have found in it almost as striking diversities as in the teeth.

But to a more practical part of our subject—the preservation of this wonderful covering, and the probability or not of its restoration. So many men engaged in the useful pursuit of cropping down the redundant locks of the public have nostrums for curing all diseases connected with whiskers and hair—and which supposed remedies are as absurd in theory as useless in practice—that people have little inclination to listen to anything broached in connection with this matter. The principal recommendation to the pomades sold by hair-cutters, and vaunted by them as being so certain in effect, is that they are elaborately got up, well perfumed, and beautiful in colour. The consistency, however, is often such, that they are the best preparations possible for producing a gloss, which is so desirable to the good appearance of the locks of both sexes. It has been our fortune to come in contact with a few men engaged in the hair-dressing vocation, whose powers of observation have led them to adopt proper measures for the restoration of hair; and it would be well if their numbers were larger, as the public would be less tormented, when undergoing the operation of hair-cutting, by senseless twaddle respecting the matter then being manipulated upon—thereby escaping a double shearing from both head and pocket. For these and similar evils the march of intellect must be the remedy; but it is hoped that the sensible hair-dresser will be appreciated, and that the foolish talking one will find his nonsense far behind the age in which we live.

It is remarkable that few persons are "perfectly bald." Most individuals who apply to themselves this appellation, or whose friends hint that they are " bald-headed," rarely examine the skin sufficiently to be able to perceive that that which they deemed without hair is covered with a fine downy substance as light as floss-silk. By the aid of the microscope, or the ordinary magnifying glass, the root of the hair can be seen under the scarf-skin; and if the examiner will take the trouble to mark out a square inch upon that part of the head on which the hair has become deficient, and count by the assistance of his glass the number of roots, and then compare the number to that upon a healthy part of the scalp, he will be surprised to find that there is very little difference. We say a healthy part of the skin advisedly, for when the hair falls the cause is in the skin, and the functions of it must be performed properly before that which grows from it, and is wholly dependent upon it, can be healthful. In extreme old age, and in cases of protracted illness, the root of the hair may be destroyed; in such instances it is worse than useless to apply anything, or adopt any measures for its recovery. When it is found that the root is still existing, the first thing to be done for a successful termination of one's efforts in recovering what we all so much value, is to choose the sensible hair-cutter we have mentioned above, and explain to him that we require him to cut every hair upon our head. We shall not be satisfied by his carefully combing up the longest of our hairs and tipping them, but what we insist upon is that, not only will he cut the long, but the short hair, or what may be called—not forgetting the analogy we have established—the undergrowth. With all persons there is more or less of this short hair growing amongst the longer, and from its being weak, it is quite important that it be cut, that it may become stronger from this treatment.

Finding by a close examination that our meagre patches are not literally free from the germ, we should rub into the skin once in every twenty-four hours the Cantharides Oil, that the skin may perform its functions with a greater degree of regularity than that part of it has done hitherto. Get the skin healthy, and there will be little to prevent all connected with it being strong and luxuriant. It may be thought somewhat unfortunate that the writer of this paper should be proprietor of the far-famed Cantharides Oil, as it would appear to his advantage pecuniarily to dwell upon this part of the subject with mingled feelings. It is perhaps undesirable, but the circumstance has arisen through the close connection that exists in the discovery of an article for increasing the quantity and quality of the hair, and the interest the discoverer would naturally take in the subject now treated.

In order that the Cantharides, or any other preparation, may be fully successful, and that the skin may be more susceptible to its influence, it is recommended that the head be washed with warm water once every ten days. By this means the old grease, and confined or rancid perspiration, are removed from the skin; anything like foetid matter is destroyed; and thus the stimulating oil is unimpeded in its influence.

The attempt to recover the hair will be disappointed if the experimentist uses the Cantharides according to the formula of the Pharmacopœia. Although the preparations therein mentioned are exciting to the skin, there are influences connected with their action which are not beneficial for the purpose. For instance, the *Tincture*, as everybody knows, is prepared with spirits of wine, and from this very fact the inaptibility is apparent; as it will not only tend to dry the skin by its ready evaporation, but from its drying tendency will quickly turn the hair grey. What is greyness? Loss of natural colour; and this colour is a fluid that, when the hair is healthy, circulates as does the sap in a tree. If you dry up or exhaust this fluid, you are grey; and for this reason it is desirable—yes, necessary—to eschew all preparations with spirit in them.

SUPERFLUOUS HAIR ON THE FACE, ARMS AND FOREHEAD.

By ALEX. ROSS, M.A.

I introduce this subject by remarking that persons with superfluous hair on the upper lip and chin, are often so distressed with its appearance, that they despair of happiness of life, and even go so far as to wish their life was at an end. One would hardly suppose it possible that a few hairs more or less should produce a state of mind bordering on insanity; but so it is, and not a very long time back I came in contact with a person who expressed herself in this way, that if the hairs on the chin and upper lip were not removed, self destruction would follow. It is a very remarkable thing that such distress should be caused by a condition of hair, which, in some countries, is not cared for at all, and, indeed, often thought to be an ornament in every woman's face. Such, however, is the power of fashion, and this goddess has much to answer for. It may be well said, that what is in excess at one time is a superfluity at another. In the southern countries, the ladies strive as hardly to have a moustache as English women do to annihilate hair on the face. The Turk scrapes and shaves his head to make room for his turban, whilst the French and English use Ross's Cantharides to increase the hair upon their heads and faces. The athletic encourage a florid and healthy complexion, whilst the gallant, as also the lady, use preparations to reduce the coarse and unrefined look of what is greatly admired by the æsthetic—the marble tint. It is so in the provision of nature. A dearth at one time, and a superabundance at another. The inhabitants of the sea are few and small now and again, at other times plentiful and extremely superfluous. It is no uncommon thing to find young ladies with such a profusion of hair, that they resort to the cutting of it close to the head near the crown, combing the long hair that is left over the comparatively bald but now cool part, this is a superfluity which, as they get older, they do not have, and so with the shaven and shorn face of the young man, the growth is found to be profuse in early days, but time acts as a "Depilatory," gradually removing and destroying strong and robust hair growth. Among the curious things I have known, seen, and read of in connection

* Note.—Liquid for Black Specks, 3s. 6d, and 5s. 6d. per bottle, sent free for 36 and 54 postage stamps.

with superfluous hair, the following may perhaps be interesting :—I have
seen it growing inside the lid of the eye, necessitating a careful operation
its frequency being according to its speed of growth, for "Depilatory"
would be of no service in such a case as this. In the mouth
hair will grow, as also in the nostrils and ears; in the latter,
the "Hair Destroyer,"* alias Depelatory, is often used, and it
is a successful remedy. In hospitals, this Depilatory is used
to the heads and faces of patients, for it removes the hair quickly
without distressing the patient; and as it takes a few applications to
entirely destroy the root of hair, one application can do but little harm
to a man's beard or to a woman's thick and long hair. Some of my
patients in their excessive feeling—their great excitement, rejoice greatly
when they find the strong stubborn hair removed, and the bearded face
made in appearance like the palm of the hand; and they are equally cast
down when they find that the vigorous root of hair is endeavouring to
recover itself and demanding that the hair *shall* live. Excitable people
have little reasoning powers while excited, and when it is argued that if
one application of the "Depilatory" checks the growth and makes it a
question, in some cases, as to whether the root shall have vigour enough
to again show its stems—that if once using does this, then two and more
must eventually give total destruction; that is to say, if one application
really injures, what will the enemy do when it has been so treated half
a dozen times. Yea, more! some people (and I see some of every
charact/ristic) are so impatient in their requests that they challenge me
to destroy the hair there and then. This *can* be done, and I will here
give some particulars. Things and actions done in haste are seldom done
well, but yet, I do suggest in some cases of superfluous hair that a
cauterizing of the hair be adopted. It is painful, and if not carried out
with care will mark the skin for a time. The process is this. A liquid
of a peculiar appearance, of marked and strong character, is applied
separately to *each* root in this way: a pointed iron stem is dipped into
the fluid, and then by the aid of a magnifying glass each root is seen, and
should be slightly touched with this burning and destructive liquid;
pain like the prick of a pin follows, whilst the destructive process is
going on, then all is over, and the satisfaction is that one root of hair is
killed never more to tease and tantalize by its increase of size day after
day. This treatment is repeated until all share the same fate. It is a
tedious doing in the extreme, but its process is written here to show those
people who challenge me that hair may be and is destroyed most
speedily. I may add, that to the better carrying out of this treatment a
magnifying mirror is often used, and such is of great service, as by looking at one's self in such a glass, the very pores of the skin may be seen.
Should further information be required by the reader in this particular,
I should be very happy to reply to queries, provided they are accompanied with a stamped envelope for their answering.

It is a painful thing to see, as I have seen, a young and handsome
maiden with the hair of the forehead meeting that of one eyebrow, contrasting sadly with the other as it is perfect in form, colour, and quantity.
Much discretion is required in a case like this. The hair generally is
very strong, and the "Depilatory" in removing hair should be so used
as not to so thoroughly remove it as to leave a line of demarcation, for
if you observe, nature does not suddenly commence the growth of hair

---

* See advertisement of Alex. Ross' Hair Destroyer or Depilatory.

upon the head round the forehead with a thick production, but graduates
it from a single hair up to an innumerable quantity. Persons to remove
hair from over the temples to give an intellectual appearance, often leave
a line of demarcation that is not pleasant to see.

The bearded lady we hear so much about is not the novelty most
people think. I have seen many, and have had the privilege of advising
for the removal of their disfigurement. These persons are greatly pleased
to have their faces as others, and the principal regret perhaps is, that
they had not been earlier informed as to a remedy. As is well known,
there is a great diversity of hair, not only in colour but in texture, and
the treatment is equally diversified, In most cases the following is the
modus operandi :—Ross' Depilatory is put into a saucer, the quantity
being not more than would cover a five shill'ng piece ; by the aid of a
little cold water this is made into a paste. It is taken between the thumb
and finger and smeared over the skin where the hair is a disfigurement.
There is no fear of the skin being affected, and therefore it is left doing
its work for five or six minutes ; then, by the aid of a wet cloth, it is
wiped from the skin. What then ? the hair has gone, the skin is free,
and if the hair has not been plucked, cut, burned, or in any way tampered with previous to its use, the probabilities are that it will not
appear again, or at worst, require no more than another application.

I have again and again seen the hands of even delicate people
covered with hair, focusing itself between fingers, more particularly the index finger and thumb, there growing longer and
darker. One application of the preparation I have been speaking
of is enough to kill for ever such hair; of course there must
have been no previous treatment in the way of burning or cutting, but a
fair case, showing justly the wonderful power of this celebrated compound imitated by many but exacted by none. I have in my avocation
seen many distressing cases of disfigurement by surplus hair, but never
knew of one but has been mitigated or entirely relieved from its excessive
mental torment by using means such as I have described.

THE EXPERIENCE OF ONE USING ALEX.

ROSS'S HAIR-COLOUR WASH.

By ALEX. ROSS, LL.D.

FOR some few years past I have been made painfully aware that I am
looking less fresh, less young, and less comely, indeed, my *reflections*
have told that I am more *obese*, or more set, as friends tell me. I am also
compelled to perceive that my skin is less elastic, is more cloudy and
wrinkled in cheek and forehead. And if I could persuade myself that all
these indicate development only, I err ; for considering that I am nearing
fifty, common-sense tells me it is age, and that the arrival at development
has passed some ten years ago. Now, as I find my buoyancy of spirits
good, my health perfect, and as I am in the full enjoyment of life, I confess
that these indications of time annoy me, and I cannot give way readily.
This being the case, I have tried to remedy these matters, remove these
imperfections. In some I have been easily successful, in others I have had
more difficulty. For instance, obesity gave me trouble to overcome, while
an improvement in complexion I have accomplished by the use of skin
tonic and other preparations.

The great indication of time, and one that for a considerable while, over-came me, was grey hair and whiskers, and it is my experience with these matters that I am desirous of recounting to my readers.

When a few grey hairs showed themselves on my temples, on the nape of my neck, with a sprinkling of silver in my beard and moustache, I suc-ceeded in hiding them by the use of a little dark cosmétique. It is true that my shirt-collar and front required the wash-tub oftener, on account of its use, and that I had to use coloured pocket-handkerchiefs instead of white—no small drawback, as I have always had as strong a feeling for white garments as ever could any negro. The monster Time, however, soon beat me, and I soon found that black cosmétique was a mistake. Several of my friends had used preparations for colouring the hair with more or less success, and I was determined to apply to one of our best per-fumers and dealers in the preparations for something that would prove permanent, and that could be applied with little trouble. A house-surgeon, a friend of mine—a man of quick discernment in all matters pertaining to the body, whether for health or appearance—soon discovered that the Hair-Colour Wash* was competent for producing all that could be wanted for such persons as myself, and his zeal was not small in his investigations, as he also was a man fast losing good appearance. He was a fair man, and had retained a somewhat youthful look up till fifty years, but then greyness set in with a vigour that baffled the art of the physician and sur-geon, so that until he found the Hair-Colour Wash he despaired of ever looking young again. No sooner was he convinced of its goodness than he used it, and in a few hours his hair assumed all the freshness and youthful look it had had before. It was the effect produced on this man by this marvellous preparation that caused the writer to resort to it, and he states, without fear of contradiction, that any person, let his hair be ever so grey, can in twelve hours see former colour, gloss, and beauty return. A man in middle life, who has mixed and been with the world day after day with-out intermission, is not easily surprised, whether it be an unexpected declaration of war, the breaking-out of an epidemic, or a conflagration, but I confess when I saw that greyness which had been years steadily coming on me, and which I had worked hard to suppress, gradually answer to a liquid, simple in look as water drawn from a well, I confess that my astonishment was about equal to my delight; and you may be sure this was not small, to a man who thought he was in appearance confirmedly old, while in life and limb he felt young. Carefully and slowly did I pass the damp brush through my hair, then the comb, after which, on went my spectacles, that I might get a more careful inspection of results. And sure enough, there was the effect; the dreadful white hair was less white, and the appearance of old age was indeed lessening. I had been informed that in twenty-four hours at most every grey hair would disappear, and cer-tainly long before half that time had expired I had ridded myself of most of my whiteness, both in the head and face. It is the case, that success in little matters often pleases us as much as it does in larger ones, and I assure the reader that my succeeding in this particular produced as much satisfaction in my mind as did anything I can recollect. I had before been gratified with the results produced on my hair with dark cosmétique, for

* This article is sold, at 10s. 6d., there being enough for this sum to last 12 months, and even more, for a careful user.

they had covered over the greyness; but there was always the unpleasantness of finding, when I passed my hand over my beard, a black, greasy mass to come where it was not wanted. Not so with the preparation now before me. Here was a beautifully-perfumed Wash, which I poured into my wash-basin, and then dipping my greasy hair-brush into it, I damped my hair, producing refreshing and cooling effects, culminating in a desire to reapply the liquid, if it were only for the agreeable sensation it produced. Not only this, but it tightened my hair, which before was somewhat loose and falling. It produced a gloss, and altogether gave me, in colour and beauty, such an ornament for my head as I had never had before.

This is a disbelieving age, and we wonder whether we shall be believed in the statement we have made. We are not induced to find fault with the public for not readily taking for granted statements of this kind; for we are aware that there are many preparations now sold with pretensions for metamorphosing grey heads which do not do so; but if we offer to give any grey one positive proof of the good results of this preparation, we shall put ourselves in a position creditable to us and advantageous to the public; and, therefore, to this end we say that any individual, at almost any convenient time, can see one or more persons at Mr. Alex. Ross's establishment whose hair has or is undergoing the change by this wonderworking liquid. Let us be understood. Either the proprietor, some of his staff, or customers, are generally to be found at 248 High Holborn, who will give any persons interested an opportunity of seeing what the Hair-Colour Wash will effect for greyness in less than twelve hours.

ALEX. ROSS'S APHORISMS.

I.—I was forcibly struck with the bad appearance greyness gives to the head and face as I presented myself for examination for a certain office, of which it is of no importance that the reader should be acquainted. The examination was before a board of gentlemen, all past middle-life, and who, from their absorbing pursuits, evidently paid little attention to anything ornamental. The room in which they sat was a long one, with large windows facing the doorway at which I entered. The examiners, all grey-headed men, sat with their backs to the light, which, from its being a brilliant day, was unusually powerful. It was this strong light, and the unlucky position of the greys, that produced an effect most extraordinary to behold. Each man appeared to have a halo surrounding his face and head, produced by the white transparent hair that grew round his chin and above his forehead. In the eagerness of debate the old worthies had thrust their fingers through their locks to such an extent that their hair stood on end, "like quills upon the fretful porcupine," thus rendering the effect more striking. These men, although not given to ornament and show, very well knew the pleasures of good living, and this was pretty palpable from their portly frames and red, jolly faces. I had well primed myself for a serious tussle in things intellectual, and felt somewhat nervous as to whether my mind would serve me as well in an examination before twenty persons as it had done when I examined myself. This I

* The Hair-Curling Fluid is sold in large bottles at 3s. 6d. Customers ordering from the country can have it forwarded by rail. It is our custom to send our preparation by post, but this article being weighty, it is better forwarded by rail. Post-office orders or stamps in payment are willingly accepted from our patrons

began to doubt, and the very doubting produced an uneasiness which was ill-calculated to produce favourable results. I had, however, no sooner entered the room, and obtained a full view of my red-faced and illuminated examiners, than my fear departed, leaving me to contend with rising laughter difficult to conceal. The more I looked at the men opposite me the brighter and more lustrous they looked. And when a short, much-haired individual addressed me, as a commencement, it was with difficulty I could give him a serious reply. One or two of the board had a predilection for scratching one particular part of the head more than another, rendering the hair that favoured that spot restless and more dishevelled, causing it to break the outline, and thus give an unorthodox halo, which was comical in the extreme. The greyness of the men, and the action of the strong light on it, aided by the position in which they had placed themselves, was the cause of my success in passing a severe ordeal; for by these agencies my mind was brought from a state of tremor to one of ease, and even jollity, which rendered me capable of answering questions of a character that required a state of mind other than morbidly serious.

II.—Nothing is more easy than to be able to comprehend how that an astringent acts upon a skin from which the hair is falling. For it is only necessary to recollect that when the teeth loosen, an astringent wash will act upon the gums in such a way as to tighten the teeth. Let this be an illustration to a few who pooh-pooh the possibility of preventing their hair falling off.

III.—Some people are extravagant in all things. Not only in eating, drinking, and spending money, but in their toilet. Cosmétiques should be used with artistic taste; they thus produce elegance without showiness. A touch here and there to the face, hands, and hair will produce a better effect than daubing it over a large surface. Seldom should extreme black be used in dye; never perfectly white enamel; not often more than a little liquid rouge to the prominent part of the cheek. Eye-colour always moderately, and powder in such small quantity that it is not suspected.

IV.—Nothing can be more vexatious than to find one has dyed one's hair black instead of brown. This may be prevented by care in the purchase, and observing the character of the dye marked on its case.

V.—It is an old adage—"A penny wise and a pound foolish." This is illustrated in people making their own Hair Dye, Curling Fluid, and Depilatories.

VI.—Medical men can give very little good advice respecting diseases of the hair. It is accounted for in this wise. Men engaged in curing and relieving patients of diseases painful to endure, cannot bring their minds to attend to that which principally affects good appearance.

VII.—It is often remarked that if there were any preparation that would with certainty cure baldness, those in high life with little hair would apply it. And such would be the case, and their baldness would be removed, *if they but heard* of the remedy. But they often do not, and persons less favoured in means are often acquainted with sources of cure which the rich from their exalted position are unable to know.

VIII.—It is an error to believe that in making the hair a light colour the original shade must be so reduced as to be strikingly apparent. Solarine used for the purpose may be so diluted as to produce any degree of lightness.

IX.—It is a fact that you can get the best articles only from certain localities, as the finest whisky from Scotland and Ireland, and the best Hair Preparations from Ross's in High Holborn.

X.—"Why is every lady so fond of beauty?" was asked of Aristotle. He replied, "This must be the question of a blind man." The wisdom of this reply would be perceived in a moment if the change could be seen worked upon an ugly person by the coiffeur.

XI.—The difference that exists between comely and uncomely appearance is principally obtained by improving the appearance of the eye, which is done by the use of Eye-Colour. By improving the complexion by the aid of Skin Tonic—the teeth by proper powders—the lips with suitable salve—the hair by dyes and washes, and the nose by studying the directions given for the form of its cartilage. (See Ross's *Toilet Magazine.*)

XII.—Great have been the improvements made in cosmétiques of late years. Pigments for the skin in these days are prepared so that they do not easily come off. Not so in days far remote. Martial tells us that the Roman ladies were afraid of the rain, on account of it producing an unfavourable appearance to the chalk with which they used to cover their faces.

XIII.—It is supposed that a Yankee has ugly hair, is a bad figure, and has legs without calves. However true this may be in some instances, we know of many New-Yorkers whose figure, hair, and legs cannot be surpassed for good appearance. It is a proverb that the young ladies of America excel their cousins in beauty. How far this may be attributed to their more frequent use of toilet requisites I cannot say, but this I know, they do not hesitate to use any *good* article for the purpose, while in this country ladies are not easily persuaded into the use of cosmétiques.

XIV.—A half-pint bottle of Skin Tonic (Alex. Ross's) is sold for 3s. 6d. It is by far the best preparation that can be used. It is such an astringent and healer of the skin as has never, perhaps, been before the public, and yet in the face of all this I here give a receipt gratis for a complexion Wash. I do so because it is a good one, and because there are many of my fair friends who cannot feel justified in an outlay of 3s. 6d. upon an article of luxury. Take emulsion of bitter almonds, half-a-pint; sal ammonia, half a drachm; and one dram of oxmuriate of quicksilver. This may be used twice or three times daily.

THE ART OF ENAMELLING THE SKIN.—Every compound supplied and the fullest directions given for the process by Alex. Ross, 21, Lamb's Conduit Street, London, W.C. Letters replied to. Ross's Cantharides for hair growth.

SPANISH FLY is the acting ingredient to Alex. Ross's Cantharides Oil, which speedily produces whiskers and thickens hair, 3s. 6d.; sent by post for P.O. Order, 4s. Advice verbally or written, fee 5s. Letters by return.

GREY HAIR.—Alex. Ross dyes hair a very light or very dark colour, permanently. Charges moderate. Dye sold at 10s. 6d., 5s. 6d., and 3s. 6d. Easily applied. Sent post for 54, 84, and 144 stamps. Send piece of hair for pattern.

CELEBRATED PREPARATIONS,

INVENTED AND SOLD BY
ALEX. ROSS,

(Editor of Ross's TOILET MAGAZINE, and Perfumer to many Distinguished Person

---

ALEX. ROSS'S LIQUID HAIR DYE.—It is most easy of application, it being merely necessary to damp the hair with it, by the aid of a comb or brush; producing an extreme light brown, a dark brown, or black colour permanently. It is sold at 3s. 6d., 5s. 6d., 10s. 6d., and 21s. per bottle; or sent upon receipt of stamps to the amount.

ALEX. ROSS'S HAIR DESTROYER OR DEPILATORY.—It removes superfluous hair from the face, neck, arms, or hands, without the slightest injury to the skin. The prices are 3s. 6d., 5s. 6d., 10s. 6d., and 21s By post for 54, 84, or 144 stamps. The largest size is sent per rail.

SPANISH FLY is the acting ingredient in ALEX. Ross's **CANTHA-RIDES OIL.** It is a sure Restorer of Hair, and a Producer of Whiskers. Its effect is immediate. It is patronised by Royalty. The prices of it are the same as the above-mentioned articles.

ALEX. ROSS'S HAIR CURLING FLUID.—It curls immediately straight and ungovernable Hair. It is of no consequence how straight or ungovernable the hair is when it is used. Sold at 3s. 6d. and 5s. 6d. Sent for 54 and 84 stamps.

ALEX. ROSS'S SKIN TONIC improves the Complexion by once using, and by continuing its use, a brilliant appearance to the skin is obtained. Sold at 5s. 6d. per bottle, or sent by post for 84 stamps. By its use pimples, discolourations, and all imperfections of the skin are removed.

ALEX. ROSS'S BLOOM OF ROSES produces a colour to the cheeks which is perfectly natural in appearance. Price 3s. 6d.; sent for 54 stamps.

ALEX. ROSS'S FACE POWDER.—1s.; sent for 14 stamps.

ALEX. ROSS'S PIMPLE REMOVER.—All Skin Diseases are improved by one dose of the VEGETABLE SKIN PILL. They produce a transcendent complexion. Price 2s. 9d. and 7s. 6d.; sent for 40 or 100 stamps.

ALEX. ROSS'S ENAMEL.—The Skin may be made transcendently beautiful by Enamelling. The process is most simple, requires no preparation, and can be easily done by one's self in a few minutes. Scars, freckles, wrinkles, and all imperfections hidden. Full directions with each packet. Price 10s. 6d.; sent for 144 stamps.

WONDERFUL DISCOVERY.—Corns cured in one day, by using ALEX. Ross's CHIROPO. This preparation gradually dissolves the Corn in a few hours, removing the very root. Price 4s.; sent by post for 60 stamps.

HAIR COLOUR WASH.—By merely damping the Hair with this elegantly-perfumed Hair Wash two or three days consecutively, the hair becomes its original colour, which is retained by an occasional using of the Wash. Price 10s. 6d.; sent for the amount in stamps.

Celebrated Inventions, &c.

PREPARED AND SOLD BY

ALEX. ROSS, M.A., LL.D.

EAR MACHINE.—This instrument has the characteristic, that it gives the exact amount of Pressure required to making the ears properly positioned. Price 10s. 6d., sent for 6d extra, secretly packed.

ENLARGED TOE JOINTS.—By the use of a compress well saturated with a liquid known as Ross' Preparation for Enlarged Joints, great relief and goodness of shape is obtained. 3s. 6d. per bottle.

FINGER SHAPERS.—These are small instruments in which the points of the fingers are laid, and then pressed into good shape, by which the nails and the points of the fingers are quickly beautified. 3s. 6d.

OVER-STOUTNESS is dispersed by carrying out regulations as given by Alex. Ross. A certain alteration for the better is made in 14 days, as may be tested by weighing from time to time. Fee 5s.

MAGNETO ELECTRIC MACHINE.—May be used with the greatest success for stopping the hair from falling, and for increasing its growth. Price 21s.

HIP BANDS.—For forming the Hips that are squatty and inelegant into good shape. Price 21s.

SPLINTS FOR BOW LEGS, IN-GROWING KNEES, and for FEET and LIMBS not quite straight and well-portioned. 10s. 6d. and 21s.

FLORID COMPLEXION toned down by using astringent liquids to the skin. 3s. 6d. per bottle.

KNEE CAPS, for pressing in the knees, and thus lengthening the limbs, giving height, commonly called tallness.

TATTOO MARKS, and all marks removed from the skin, by using a Bleaching Liquid, which is quite harmless. It takes the colour from Moles, &c. Price 3s. 6d.

ARTIFICIAL NOSES.—Persons not able to visit Mr. Ross on account of distance, can have them made to perfection, by sending Photo, and a few particulars as to complexion and age. Price two guineas.

A SIMPLE CONTRIVANCE FOR IMPROVING THE FIGURE by drawing back the shoulders, and Expanding the Chest, price 7s. 6d., by post, 7s. 9d.

EYE COLOUR is a preparation for Dressing the Eye. It consists of three Preparations, one for the eyebrows and lash, another for giving seeming size to the organ, and one for hiding any marks around it. The second preparation is of a peculiar blue character, which is put amongst the hair of the lower lash, producing a wonderful effect, 3s. 6d. or 54 stamps

ALEX. ROSS' TOILET MAGAZINE is full of Toilet Secrets, 1s., or 14 stamps.

TOOTH POWDER, for taking from the teeth the yellow tint that so unsightly, 2s. 6d., post, 34 stamps.

A TONIC MEDICINE for giving hilarity of spirits, and a permanent animated tone to the feature, 5s. 6d., sent by post for 70 stamps.

GOLDEN HAIR WASH, for making the darkest hair of a beautiful golden or light tint. It can be so used, that any amount of lightness may be obtained, 5s. 6d. and 10s. 6d., sent for 70 and 144 stamps.

A HAIR COLOURER IN ONE LIQUID, 4s. and 10s. 6d. per bottle.

THE FOUNDATION OF PIECES OF HAIR WORN ON BALD PLACES, is made of a material strong and transparent. Upon giving an order for these, send pattern of hair, and size of bald place.

CHIN AND CHEEK IMPROVERS. (*see Ross's Pamphlet upon this.*) Shape produced by pressure upon the cartilage existing beneath the skin.

THE NOSE MACHINE, used now by the public for ten or twelve years, 10s. 6d., post, secretly packed for 10s. 6d.

FEET IMPROVED IN FORM, the Toes Straightened, and the Ankles strengthened. The appliances worn during the night or any leisure time.

Advice given upon personal appearance to any one requiring such, verbally, or by letter. Fee, 5s.

A RED NOSE.—Nothing mars the appearance so much as this does. A remedy, with full directions, sent for 5s. in stamps.

KHOUL, for giving Colour to the Eyelashes and Corners of the Eye. 5s. 6d., free by post.

GIPSY.—A preparation in both powder and liquid form, for darkening the skin. It gives the Gipsy, or the Spanish colour to the skin. The Italian and Eastern complexion may be had by its use. 5s. 6d., 10s. 6d. and 21s.

THE TEMPORARY COVERING OF BRUISES AND MARKS OF THE SKIN, by the aid of suitable colouring, is supplied by Alex. Ross accompanied with brushes and directions. Sent free for 54 stamps.

All persons having imperfections in personal appearance are invited to apply by letter or otherwise to Alex. Ross, when they will be supplied with the fullest information as to the removing of them at little trouble and expense. All letters are *replied to in plain envelopes* and *no printed* matter is ever put upon parcels for transit neither at home nor abroad. All letters are answered by Mr. Alex. Ross, and those to be answered promptly should have a stamped envelope.

21, LAMBS' CONDUIT STREET, LONDON.

Near the Foundling Hospital.

THE FLORID NOSE.

By ALEX. ROSS, M.A., LL.D.,

21, LAMB'S CONDUIT STREET, HIGH HOLBORN, LONDON,

(near the Foundling).

My choice of a subject to write upon generally emanates from a want among my constituents, my customers, and my friends. The want of a plan—a remedy, a device for getting rid of a red nose, and possessing one pale, cool, and marble-like, given utterance to by very many of my patients, is the reason for my now writing under the title of Florid Noses.

A florid complexion is considered inelegant, and no lady is desirous of having a rosy face, and much less a centre feature, red, heated, and contrasting with the forehead, and it may be with the cheeks and chin. Such is the dislike to a red nose that I am inquired of, more for a means of ridding the *élite* of society from this imperfection than I am to enable them to obtain the means to remove imperfections of more common possession, and those one would suppose of far greater inconvenience.

"I am very good looking, young, and possessed of unusually well shaped features," are the remarks of correspondents to me; "but," they add, "my nose is a trial to me, every now and again, when I wish, it may be looking its best, my centre feature will become red—will feel hot, and will give me no end of discomfort, will render me nervous and possess me with the idea that my florid look is as noticeable as the red at any point of danger."

The distress produced by this condition of the face is suffered from by both sexes, irrespective of age, figure, or complexion. Of course the young object to it the most, but men of forty and women of thirty are greatly annoyed by their appearance and feelings when their noses are redder than is usual when they are with their friends and acquaintances. Many a fair lady wishes she were of dark complexion, for then the unduly coloured feature would be less conspicuous; and not a few men envy their dark skinned brothers, as thus the member made ugly by its colour would look less unsightly, and they would be less nervous and uncomfortable. Let a woman be ever so beautiful, or a man never so handsome, this one imperfection is more than enough to render the face the opposite to a condition of good looks. Only say a person has a red nose, and it is equivalent to describing them as uncomely and inelegant. The pale nose, it is said, is peculiar to the aristocracy, and that there is much in the shape of the member in distinguishing the plebeian from the aristocrat; but perhaps more distinguishing is the colour—the redder the feature, the lower in the grade of class, is generally believed. Such being the belief, can it be wondered at that people make themselves uncomfortable who have a member so *distingué* as is black from white. Talking once to a worthy medical man, he gave utterance, among many things, to the expression of dissatisfaction he felt in many cases in which he could do no good, whilst I, reminded him that there were others that derived so much from his skill, that they must more than compensate for what he was unable to accomplish. And so it is, to some degree, with the remedies for the florid nose; in some extreme cases I am pained to find that the cure is remote, but I have the pleasurable feeling to know that in all cases an amelioration comes, and then follows a large proportion of perfect riddance of this distressing malady.

Perhaps to no part of the face does an artist give more care—a greater number of touches and retouches than the nose. If he produce handsomeness of man and beauty of women, the nose is well formed and of uniform colour; so also if he would give the beholders of his creation the idea that such was of intellectual character, the centre feature would be pale and of paleness not varied. A true Grecian nose is straight, small, and of perfect whiteness. The forehead should in beauty be white, but the nose should be still whiter. The rounded aristocratic member is large, but how noticeably pale, how free from coarseness, how exempt from unevenness and redness. The thought comes to many, that as they can make their hands free from redness and can give them evenness and paleness, why not do as much for the feature in question. It may be well asked, for it is one of those incongruities which when thought of puzzle us. But more upon the means of cure presently. The Hungarian nose, as also the Italian, is noticeable for its pallor. The Scotch and English are not so well favoured. The Turk has a colour to the nose which suits well the complexion; whilst the French have often as ugly a tint as any Esquimaux. It is well to put the reader into possession of the characteristics of this feature, that it may be more readily understood how to treat the several cases so often met with by myself and seen by everyone mixing in society. The fleshy nose is nearly always more or less red, and it is one of the most difficult to cure. The more cartilaginous the feature, the whiter and better shaped is it.; if it be fleshy, the circulation of the blood is more or less apparent, whilst with cartilage there is little or no blood circulation, and as blood is the redness and non-circulation is the opposite, the cause and effect is palpable.

A blue nose is often to be seen in cold weather; it is produced also by illness, such as biliousness and juandice, but if a gristley feature, little of it is seen, for it is only fleshy conditions retain their colour. I never recollect reading of blue noses in the classics, for the Greeks and Romans had hard, well chiselled nasal organs, and such are delineated in the statuary to be seen in our museums. If there be rulers, be they emperors, queens or kings, generals, captains or drill sergeants, they lose cast and power over their subordinates if their *leading article* be not as a Wellington, or Napoleon, and Lavater says that an arched nose indicates wit, and a blunt or fleshy one the contrary. He further says, " a beautiful nose will never be found accompanying an ugly countenance. An ugly person may have fine eyes, but not a handsome nose," for the handsome member gives excellence to the whole countenance. Surely it behoves us to do our best to keep this important member from undue redness, from ill shape and wrong position, and we will now show what means are employed in ridding this part of the face from so annoying a colour, so unsuitable a blazement to that part of the face that should be paler than any other.

A person unfortunate in being possessed with a soft flabby nose, is as we have hinted, more susceptible to a red condition of it than any other, for an attack of severe indigestion will make itself conspicuous by disfiguring this feature. The remedy in such a case is to give heed to the laws of health by eating and drinking carefully, and choosing the simple medicine wisely prescribed. For my own part, I think there is nothing better for this complaint than using the Magneto Electric Machine, and following a few rules which I should be happy to prescribe for my friends, and to whom I could send the Magneto Instrument. Brandy and port wine are useful, and yes! enjoyable, but the owner of the fleshy organ should drink neither, for the blood is enriched, and sent with such speedy forcible circulation, that it makes the fluid conspicuous to this part of the face of which we write. An exceedingly thin skin, possessed by most fair persons is another cause for the blood to show itself readily through its covering, and therefore I recommend that the flesh be *thickened by using an astringent*; that the pores may be tightened, and thus the skin made more opaque—or at least less transparent. This astringent liquid is applied with a piece of linen or cotton wool. One nostril is plugged with it alternately for five minutes, and this is done without inconvenience or discomfort.

The outside skin of the feature is covered with a piece of linen well saturated with the astringent. This internal and outward using soon tells upon the texture of the flesh, and resists the showing through of the hot, red, and burning fluid so incidental to all dyspeptics, those of full habit of body, and the men or women who have lived in an Indian climate. The forehead, chin and neck are, as a rule, pale in colour. Why is this; it is because the skin is drawn tightly, and little blood can flow between the skin and the cartilaginous matter. And so it would be by the using of an astringent that would draw the flesh to a normal condition. This redness is sometimes caused by a tendency to an overflow of blood to the head. This is of rare occurrence, and which we should suggest be immediately put under the care of medical experts. For nervousness and indigestion, I should be glad to suggest a remedy to those who are suffering, and who would write me particulars. Too much iron in the system can be easily reduced by proper medicines, this being often the cause of excessive redness. Some people have too much of that that other people lack, and it is such who, if their features are predisposed to a florid state, show this malady off the sooner.

Of course any one having a knowledge of pathology could assign many conditions of health that could produce a flow of blood to the head, reddening the features, and persons so suffering would do well to study the laws of health as a cure for their discomfort. Apoplexy, heart disease, enlargement of the liver, gout and rheumatism, all produce much or little this tendency to redness; and when such conditions of health exist, doubtless the best cure is medical advice, whilst much even in these and other cases, the plan suggested would greatly assist. There are many noses perfect in form and texture, from root to the commencement of the point, but then commences the contrast in colour, from the marble whiteness to the excessive redness. Being an observant man in this matter, I have seen of late, during a month's east wind, most marked cases of this kind. A north wind does much in this way, but an easterly one a deal more. Had the skins of these proboscis been less porous, less redness would have presented itself, and much distress of mind would have been spared.

BLACK SPECKS, FRECKLES AND WHITE PARASITES IN THE SKIN, MORE PARTICULARLY THE FACE.

BY ALEX. ROSS, M.A.

21, LAMB'S CONDUIT STREET, LONDON.

To readily perceive how distressing is an accumulation of black specks upon the face, accompanied it may be with a larger number of yellow ones, we must bethink ourselves of the delightful effect produced by a clear complexion, a face free of blemish, and unfrequented by redness, blackness or yellow tint. Such a meditation, such a conception of what we would like our countenances to be would render emphatic force to the contrast, and give us a desire intense to remove if we have them the black parasites in the centre of the face, and the yellow specks from the whole of it, and do all that is possible to possess a clear skin and a healthy looking face. Hitherto little has been done to cure the skin of this imperfection, and when medical men have been appealed to in the matter, they have simply prescribed medicine of a trivial character, formulas of which are stereotyped in the Pharmacopœia. One of the great causes of my looking into the matter and studying the prognosis of this troublesome condition of the skin has been the displays of trouble endured by those afflicted with these tiresome imperfections in personal beauty. I have seen handsome faces spoiled by these frequent visitors. I have had questions asked me out of number for a remedy. I have seen the delightful marble pale complexion rendered sad to look upon by the black specks in hundreds, and the freckles in double their number. As I have intimated, the appeals for a remedy have been many, and therefore it induced me to give study to conquer the knowledge necessary to rid the face of that which mars beauty, as much or more than anything else among the contingencies beauty is subject to, and I am quite certain the information I am now giving will be of service if it only be in preventing the uninformed of the bad result following the usual way resorted to for the removal of these yellow and black specks, for the face is frequently rendered, I was going to say, irreclaimably spoiled, by the rough manner in which the specks are removed. At least, when the specks are ejected by pinching and pressing holes are left in the flesh that never fill up, but tend to make the skin indented and sadly uneven. It has been a matter of controversy between the healing fraternity as to whether the parisites found in the faces of human beings are indicative of a disease existing in the blood, or whether they be the disease itself. More than forty years ago, Sehonlein of Berlin, made known to the faculty that he had discovered cryptogamic vegetable forms (order Fungi) on the surface of the body, and which was simultaneous with certain skin diseases. And numerous were his disciples in this, for Doctors Jenner, Gull, Bennett of Scotland, as also Graby, Remak, Lauzenbech, Roben and others acquiesced. But their deductions were too speedy, and their decision incorrect, and it is now supposed that these parasites are a disease in themselves, and not dependendent for their presentation in any disease of the skin. The microscope has done much to enlighten us upon this subject, and the great microscopist Jabez Hogg, proved very much to the effect that Schonlein was in error when he asserted that these parasites were a symptom of disease, and not a disease themselves. I mention this controversy that it may be encouraging to those annoyed with black specks in the skin to know that there is no disease of the body more than the possession of these uncomfortable and unsightly parasites. My experience leads me to believe the following history of their existence. Persons fall into ill-health by irregular living or carelessness of themselves, by hereditary debility, and even by over feeding and indulgence, from this the skin becomes more or less fetid, and engenders decomposition, which is fully shown in what is called freckles, these yellow patches in the flesh by analysis, and the assistance of the microscope would show putrefaction, and then follows as a matter of nature the black parasites, and the yellow and other disagreeables on and in the skin. There is decidedly a greater tendency to unhealthiness of the skin in warm weather than in cold, and in a warm climate than in a cold one, and I take it that in the south of France and in Italy the beauties are more troubled with this misery than the bonnie lasses of Scotland, whether they be Kilts or Scots. It is generally the luxurious and the careless that suffer, and although it may not be altogether a remedy, yet it is an ameliorator: that of exercise, fresh air and judicious eating and drinking. Nitre in warm water is a good medicine, and may often be found to do what is wanted for specks. To disperse the parasites the nitre should be taken as a medicine, and used with one or two other compounds externally. These ugly marks on the face as we have intimated, show mostly in the centre of the face, but the forehead is not an unfrequent part for them to visit, and when so, any pressure to that part is most annoying. Many a man has raised his hat more often for these than from a spirit of gallantry. Such a degenerating of the blood as produces these torments should at once be seen to, and the skin ought immediately to be treated with liquids that kill the parasites that they may be at once removed, the holes in which they have been properly closed, and the complexion once again as it was heretofore. I should feel pleasure in advising in this matter where the cases are worse than is usual, for it really requires practice and attention to bring the skin to perfection when a condition of yellow and black specks abound. And here I may take the opportunity to intimate that I answer myself all correspondence. Ladies and gentlemen writing me from abroad, have equal attention. And I may further add that no envelope or parcel sent has any printing upon it; so that my communication reaches those who favour me with their letters or orders as an ordinary letter or packet free from anything that would indicate the contents. Letters that have postage stamps upon them are answered first, and when foreign letters can have an English stamp or stamps to frank their transit it is well, and they are answered with expedition, but as I know that in India, Canada and Australia, as in many other places, English stamps cannot be procured, I generally am careful not to be remiss in responding to my querist. I do hope that no lady or gentleman reading these few lines either at home or abroad will for an hour after this allow these unsightly specks to remain without making an effort to annihilate them. My reader, I invite your attention to the fact that the note below informs you of a remedy for unsightliness, discomfort and unhealthiness of the skin.*

SUPERFLUOUS HAIR ON THE FACE, ARMS AND FOREHEAD.

By ALEX. ROSS, M.A.

I introduce this subject by remarking that persons with superfluous hair on the upper lip and chin, are often so distressed with its appearance, that they despair of happiness of life, and even go so far as to wish their life was at an end. One would hardly suppose it possible that a few hairs more or less should produce a state of mind bordering on insanity; but so it is, and not a very long time back I came in contact with a person who expressed herself in this way, that if the hairs on the chin and upper lip were not removed, self-destruction would follow. It is a very remarkable thing that such distress should be caused by a condition of hair, which, in some countries, is not cared for at all, and, indeed, often thought to be an ornament in every woman's face. Such, however, is the power of fashion, and this goddess has much to answer for. It may be well said, that what is in excess at one time is a superfluity at another. In the southern countries, the ladies strive as hardly to have a moustache as English women do to annihilate hair on the face. The Turk scrapes and shaves his head to make room for his turban, whilst the French and English use Ross's Cantharides to increase the hair upon their heads and faces. The athletic encourage a florid and healthy complexion, whilst the gallant, as also the lady, use preparations to reduce the coarse and unrefined look of what is greatly admired by the æsthetic—the marble tint. It is so in the provision of nature. A dearth at one time, and a superabundance at another. The inhabitants of the sea are few and small now and again, at other times plentiful and extremely superfluous. It is no uncommon thing to find young ladies with such a profusion of hair, that they resort to the cutting of it close to the head near the crown, combing the long hair that is left over the comparatively bald but now cool part, this is a superfluity which, as they get older, they do not have, and so with the shaven and shorn face of the young man, the growth is found to be profuse in early days, but time acts as a "Depilatory," gradually removing and destroying strong and robust hair growth. Among the curious things I have known, seen, and read of in connection

---

* NOTE.—Liquid for Black Specks, 3s. 6d. and 5s. 6d. per bottle, sent free for 54 and 84 postage stamps.

with superfluous hair, the following may perhaps be interesting :—I have seen it growing inside the lid of the eye, necessitating a careful operation its frequency being according to its speed of growth, for "Depilatory" would be of no service in such a case as this. In the mouth hair will grow, as also in the nostrils and ears; in the latter, the "Hair Destroyer,"* alias Depilatory, is often used, and it is a successful remedy. In hospitals, this Depilatory is used to the heads and faces of patients, for it removes the hair quickly without distressing the patient; and as it takes a few applications to entirely destroy the root of hair, one application can do but little harm to a man's beard or to a woman's thick and long hair. Some of my patients in their excessive feeling—their great excitement, rejoice greatly when they find the strong stubborn hair removed, and the bearded face made in appearance like the palm of the hand; and they are equally cast down when they find that the vigorous root of hair is endeavouring to recover itself and demanding that the hair *shall* live. Excitable people have little reasoning powers while excited, and when it is argued that if one application of the "Depilatory" checks the growth and makes it a question, in some cases, as to whether the root shall have vigour enough to again show its stems—that if once using does this, then two and more must eventually give total destruction; that is to say, if one application really injures, what will the enemy do when it has been so treated half a dozen times. Yea, more! some people (and I see some of every characteristic) are so impatient in their requests that they challenge me to destroy the hair there and then. This *can* be done, and I will here give some particulars. Things and actions done in haste are seldom done well, but yet, I do suggest in some cases of superfluous hair that a cauterising of the hair be adopted. It is painful, and if not carried out with care will mark the skin for a time. The process is this. A liquid of a peculiar appearance, of marked and strong character, is applied separately to *each* root in this way: a pointed iron stem is dipped into the fluid, and then by the aid of a magnifying glass each root is seen, and should be slightly touched with this burning and destructive liquid; pain like the prick of a pin follows, whilst the destructive process is going on, then all is over, and the satisfaction is that one root of hair is killed never more to tease and tantalize by its increase of size day after day. This treatment is repeated until all share the same fate. It is a tedious doing in the extreme, but its process is written here to show those people who challenge me that hair may be and is destroyed most speedily. I may add, that to the better carrying out of this treatment a magnifying mirror is often used, and such is of great service, as by looking at one's self in such a glass, the very pores of the skin may be seen. Should further information be required by the reader in this particular, I should be very happy to reply to queries, provided they are accompanied with a stamped envelope for their answering.

It is a painful thing to see, as I have seen, a young and handsome maiden with the hair of the forehead meeting that of one eyebrow, contrasting sadly with the other as it is perfect in form, colour, and quantity. Much discretion is required in a case like this. The hair generally is very strong, and the "Depilatory" in removing hair should be so used as not to so thoroughly remove it as to leave a line of demarcation, for if you observe, nature does not suddenly commence the growth of hair

---

* See advertisement of Alex. Ross' Hair Destroyer or Depilatory.

upon the head round the forehead with a thick production, but graduates it from a single hair up to an innumerable quantity. Persons to remove hair from over the temples to give an intellectual appearance, often leave a line of demarcation that is not pleasant to see.

The bearded lady we hear so much about is not the novelty most people think. I have seen many, and have had the privilege of advising for the removal of their disfigurement. These persons are greatly pleased to have their faces as others, and the principal regret perhaps is, that they had not been earlier informed as to a remedy. As is well known, there is a great diversity of hair, not only in colour but in texture, and the treatment is equally diversified. In most cases the following is the *modus operandi* :—Ross' Depilatory is put into a saucer, the quantity being not more than would cover a five shilling piece ; by the aid of a little cold water this is made into a paste. It is taken between the thumb and finger and smeared over the skin where the hair is a disfigurement. There is no fear of the skin being affected, and therefore it is left doing its work for five or six minutes ; then, by the aid of a wet cloth, it is wiped from the skin. What then ? the hair has gone, the skin is free, and if the hair has not been plucked, cut, burned, or in any way tampered with previous to its use, the probabilities are that it will not appear again, or at worst, require no more than another application.

I have again and again seen the hands of even delicate people covered with hair, focusing itself between fingers, more particularly the index finger and thumb, there growing longer and darker. One application of the preparation I have been speaking of is enough to kill for ever such hair; of course there must have been no previous treatment in the way of burning or cutting, but a fair case, showing justly the wonderful power of this celebrated compound imitated by many but exacted by none. I have in my avocation seen many distressing cases of disfigurement by surplus hair, but never knew of one but has been mitigated or entirely relieved from its excessive mental torment by using means such as I have described.

CANTHARIDES AND ITS PROPERTIES AS A HAIR GROWER.

By ALEX. ROSS, LL.D.

VETERINARY Surgeons are wonderfully successful in restoring hair upon the animal, when from a fall and other causes hair disappears. What are the means resorted to to produce such effects as they do. They are merely these: Providing the root of hair exists in the case brought before them, they use plenty of water for removing all extraneous matter, and rub into the skin—that which contains the germ of hair—"Cantharides," or in other words, Spanish Fly, pulverised and mixed with fat. If there be any hair to grow, this has the desired effect, and the animal which otherwise would have lost its prestige, from having what is called technically broken knees, is restored to its former high standing among the sure-footed. The analogy existing between the four legged animal and the biped is perfect—the hair of the human being is exactly as the hair of the lower animal, save and except it is less coarse, less strong, and less plentiful. The deduction to be drawn is this, that that which will facilitate the growth of hair with one, will do so with the other, providing it is modified—reduced in strength for the use of the less strongly constituted animal, that the epidermis and cuticle of both may be treated according to texture and age. Let any person with spare hair on the face or head resort to the use of this treatment, and they will quickly find a pleasing result. I have been thus dealing with hair for more than thirty years, and I can safely say, amid all the nostrums that have sprung up during that time, I never found any to at all come up in excellence to this simple but effectual remedy.

To all appearance, the wounded skin of an animal after a severe fall seems to have been entirely divested of hair, and the inexperienced would suppose a bare ugly mark must continue until end of time with the creature. The bald head, as it is called, of many would be found on close examination not to be literally free from hair; here and there fine fluffy hair exists, and by being well supplied with "Cantharides" it fully developes, and becomes useful and ornamental, as much so as does the hair upon the knees of the horse. Indeed there are very few cases where the root of hair is destroyed, and it is more than likely that the "Cantharides," or Spanish Fly, would cover the heads of all, from the beggar to the prince. In high life and in low life there are remedies for complaints and imperfections, plentiful and close at hand, but unnoticed but by a few; and whilst there are hundreds requiring the remedy, only a few have its benefit. This is to be regretted, and I only hope that the few words I here pen may be the means of informing many what to do to cover their heads and faces with the useful and ornamental that nature once provided them with. As I have shown elsewhere, it is a bad thing to have grey hair, but to have none at all is worse, particularly as "Hair Dyes" are now so successfully used! It is not an uncommon thing to find people with the whole of the upper part of the head covered with a few fine long hairs, whilst all around appears to be barren and unprofitable. If, however, a magnifying glass be used, it will be seen that the whole of the head is thickly possessed of promising stems, and which stems, if only individually thicker and longer, would be a head of hair. It is these stems, not perceptible to the naked eye, that the Cantharides acts upon, and it is only a work of no long time to develop these sickly sprouts into luxuriant and beautiful tresses. The Spanish Fly is often used, in its almost crude state, for blistering, and such an irritant often creates hair in plenty where it is a disfigurement. A medical friend prescribed this kind of fly to the arm of a person who was apparently suffering from local rheumatism; it was used, and was successful, but a short time afterwards the limb was thickly covered with hair, it having acted upon the incipient stems hardly perceptible to the ordinary vision.

Perhaps as a rule, all dormant conditions of vegetable and animal life are altered for the better by the use of a stimulant; a torpid liver, a slow digestion, whether it exists in the intestines or in the stomach proper, a stimulant will be attended with action; and so with the growth of hair. If you excite a plant to fructify by the aid of liquids composed of properties having irritating qualities, it develops to its utmost, as also do the similarly constructed roots and stumps found upon the human head. I have often, in writing upon this subject, shown the analogy that exists between vegetation and hair—even in the planting of both. Numerous are the charlatans who profess to have secrets by which they can give a man a "heavy beard in three weeks," and a woman hair reaching the ground in as many months; but of course no thinking person would for a moment believe in these impossibilities. These impositions do much harm in preventing people giving credence when a proper and valuable remedy is brought before the public. Even with a long established concern like my own, myself and assistants are asked as to the certainty of hair being restored by applying "Cantharides." And further; I may say the ridiculous statements made by inexperienced persons whose only aim is money making, is the cause of much meagre hair, and many bald heads so frequently met with, among the young as well as the old. I will end these few words upon an important subject, that of covering the crown of the head and removing the condition of a bare face, by showing how this stimulant should be used. The scalp should be kept perfectly clean by washing twice weekly, and "Cantharides" (not the *Tincture*, as this is prepared with alcohol, which dries the root) by the aid of the points of the fingers, using a fair amount of friction to enable the skin to be well moistened with it.

The hair should be well cut monthly, and the owner should see to it that the short hair as well as the long is operated upon by the *tonsure*. One word more and I have finished. What I have been endeavouring to explain has been for the developing of hair, its growth and ultimate stability, but I have said nothing about the *falling hair*. A very different treatment is required when the locks are falling. The immediate cause of hair being easily combed from the head is, that the pores of the skin are relaxed, superinduced it may be by indisposition or violent perspiration. It is absolutely necessary to tighten the skin, that an immediate check be put upon this condition of hair and pores. To this end, let a suitable astringent powder or liquid be used, and if suitable—if different to what is prepared by careless people—the pores of the flesh will be so tightened after a few usings as to prevent the hair being easily removed, and when this is obtained then is the time to apply the "Cantharides" for expediting growth. But be sure to tighten the hair well before anything else is done. Further information upon this important treatment can be given, and the articles for its carrying out properly can be supplied at no great cost. I may be here permitted to state that I am always glad of the opportunity of giving information, by letter or otherwise, and if letters are sent me, they are replied to, generally, the following day.

GREY HAIRS, AND HOW TO GET RID OF THEM.

By ALEX. ROSS, M.A., LLD.

21, Lamb's Conduit Street, W.C., near the Foundling Hospital.

"How old you are looking!" is an expression seldom used unless grey hair is noticeable in the person so addressed, for nothing ages the appearance of an individual so much as this mark of time. Greyness is incidental to all periods of human life. Young people and old almost share alike in this It does not follow that because a person is aged that he or she should have grey hair, neither is it peremptory that because an individual is young they should be free from grey hairs. I have seen extremely old people without white looks, and I have examined the heads of beautiful children under twelve years of age with a large sprinkling of grey hair. Many young people, and more middle aged ones, who are blonde in complexion, and whose hair is fair, are grey long before they have a suspicion that such is so, for greyness lies dormant among fair locks—it is there, but is not noticed, through the resemblance it bears to its neighbours. These people eventually make the discovery, but not before they have passed the meridian of life, and then they look upon them as the true indicators of Time. Grey hair is less manageable than fully coloured. It requires more Bandoline and Fixature to keep it down—from rudely standing out as though proclaiming the status in time of its owner. It is an obstinate tell tale—hard, harsh, and rough ; and is a striking contrast to its fellows, who remain where they are placed, and have no will of their own.

This want of colour to hair, we all know, is produced by a deficiency of moisture, and which moisture is material to colour ; as with the leaf of a tree, so with the filament of our bodies ; when the winter comes it loses its moisture that has hitherto circulated through its several parts, and its colour goes ; and so when illness or deficiency of life power is affected, the material colour ceases, and we become what is called grey. Inartistic is greyness in any form, and in nature it is rarely seen, except in decay. Inelegance is concomitant with it, and beauty flees at its appearance. Oh! spare us from this canker to comeliness and personal good appearance. All who are grey can recollect the depression produced when the first grey hair was found by themselves, or was discovered for them. Doubtless many will pretend to minds too strong—too philosophic to allow they were affected by a hair free from colour, but few will believe, but their spirits were lowered many degrees by its presentation.

Some faces carry this alteration of colour better than others. A florid complexion is not so much injured by it as are others, and uniform white hair, many contend, suits a fair, florid complexion. I will allow that *white* hair has its attractions, but assert that *grey* is always more or less objectionable, while dark hair, or that without greyness or whiteness, is preferable to all, whether it be of perfect whiteness or only partially so. It may be information to some that the cause of greyness showing itself at the temples and nape of the neck soonest, is caused by the continuous application of soap to those parts. In washing the face frequently, a constant repetition of alkali is given to the temples, whilst the top of the head escapes this constant alkaline treatment ; hence the crown of the head is often free from greyness when just above the neck and cheeks the hair may be white. Perhaps the best illustration of what soap affects is, that most men after the age of forty have grey whiskers, when the hair on the head is free from the imperfection ; and yet, strange as it may appear, the latter is twenty or more years the senior of the former. Mental work, worry, and illness quickly removes colour from hair ; and although we often see a strong person with changing hair, yet the rule undoubtedly is, that the better the health, the more correct the colour. Great efforts of the mind, shocks, and surprises, tend to the fluctuation in shade : and numerous are the histories of persons hairs changing from black to white in a few hours. There is a good deal of exaggeration in the accounts, no doubt ; an instance of which comes somewhat under our notice. Some years ago a celebrated man was guillotined in France for a political offence. When taken prisoner he was of dark beard and hair, and when having been in custody for a month or two, he was noticed to be both white in face and head, and it was announced all over Europe that the terror of his position had caused his hair thus to alter. Much comment was made upon this, and physiologically the matter was gone into, and the wise pretended no surprise at the phenomenon, but expatiated upon the working of nature. We fancy they were somewhat amused when it was found that the incarcerated one had been in the habit of dyeing his hair periodically, say once every two months, and as he was hastened to his then new quarters, he had no opportunity of taking with him his superfluities, such as his Hungarian Pomade, or his Liquid Hair Dye ; hence his undressed moustache and his suddenly white hair.

But it may very naturally be asked, "What about Hair Dyes and the preparations for properly bringing hair to its colour. As greyness is disliked by all, whether ǀthey be in this country or any other, has not some good and trustful preparation been offered to the world by which the appearance of old age may be deferred. It may be said that in these days people very wisely keep off the old look, in all particulars, as long as possible ; they do not as did our grandmothers and grandfathers ; the ladies in those times, as soon as they had been married a year or two, would mount the aged-looking cap, and as soon as a grey hair appeared, would put on a black silk covering, over which would be worn the front or band, made of straight smooth hair. No, no ; a married lady remains young looking as long as she well can, and even goes beyond that time ; and the men, immediately spareness of hair or deficiency of colour supervenes, they resort to colouring, and increasing a quantity of that which gives youthful appearance to all who possess it. Our ancestors two or more generations back, knew nothing of contrivances for permanently colouring hair, and in their despair at early greyness they resorted to white powder and grease, black skull caps, and hideous fronts

or bands of hair with artificial partings. But our times are times of
advancement, and it behoves all of us to avail ourselves of opportunity
for comfort and improvement of appearance, whether it be in dress or in
using preparations for hiding grey hair, pallor of the cheek, obesity of
body, and attenuation of the same.

Many persons refrain from using Hair Dyes, simply because they bear
the strong name of dye. They would not object to apply them, providing they bore some name more elegant and less emphatic, to confess to
dyeing their hair they would abhor, but to restore its colour by the
application of Enchanted Rose Water they would have no objection to,
even though it should be in reality an instantaneous dye; this is foolish,
and we will now describe how superior a dye is to all else for hair
colour to those substitues that are colourers, but without the permanency
and good effect as to natural appearance.* It does not follow that a
good dye should consist of two preparations, one for preparing the way
for the other. Very excellent preparations are in one liquid only, and
thus saves much trouble and some time, for the first liquid has to dry
before the second is used. Neither is it necessary that the hair be quite
freed from grease in every case; and yet it is not in every case the same,
a certain light colour of the hair will admit of the hair being greasy,
and will be content with one liquid; whilst in a jet black, as black as a
Spaniard's hair, will require a dye in two liquids; but this the public
need not trouble itself about; for if they obtain the coloured dye, they
should, one or the other would be supplied, accompanied with the fullest
directions; and this leads me to a description of how to apply these
useful assistants to good personal looks. Supposing the hair to have
been got ready for the dye, either by washing or combing as the require-
ment may be. The operator divides the hair into four portions of a
lady's hair, and into two for a gentleman. Thin layers of the hair are
then taken between the fingers, and a hard brush previously wetted with
the dye is passed down the lair from root to point. Immediately the dye
touches the greyness colour comes. and all imperfection disappears. The
hair is allowed to dry, and you begin to look and to feel that you have
begun life afresh, for an improvement in appearance affects the mind so
favourably. that you look upon yourself and the world with complacency
and confidence. My space here is limited, or I would tell you more
about my dyes. I would, too, tell you what they are made of, of their
manipulation, for you would never perhaps be able to procure the ingredients, and as for getting the compound together as it should be, is quite
out of the question ; but had space permitted me, I might have referred to
the crowned heads, and many but a trifle in status below them, who lux-
uriate in beautiful colours, and therefore possess all the advantages of a
pleasing appearance, not only being spared the annoyance of inferiority
in looks, but to have the pleasure, the confidence, and self-possession of
being even superior in personal elegance to any around them. I might
have shown to you more fully the folly of neglecting the use of these
extraordinary preparations, of the sacrifice made of the pleasures of this
life, in admitting of old age to come upon those barely forty or forty-
five. I might further have dealt with the subject from a mental point
of view, and shown you how exhilirated the spirits become, how peace-
ful and contented so trivial a thing as the hair being one colour instead
of another makes the mind, rendering life enjoyable, and giving one

---

* Alex Ross' Dye is for either an exceeding light or very dark colour. In
giving orders for the same, a piece of hair as pattern of colour should be sent.
Correspondence on the subject is invited.

strength to overcome difficulties and to obtain ardent wishes. Let, then, all grey-whiskered men, and every white-headed women, or those with a tendency thereto, accept my invitation to apply a small quantity of the genuine dye to their hair. They need not colour all that is grey. Let them test the liquids, if they choose, upon a hundred or more hairs, and I guarantee that they will so treat the whole, not leaving a spot untouched Persons abroad can have the light, very light, dark, very dark colours sent them by post and in the provinces the parcels post would convey to them speedily, and without observation, the parcel that would have within that that pleases all, for Time's llooks would be overcome, and early days, as it were, be enjoyed once more by its use.

"BEAUTY IS BUT SKIN DEEP."

By ALEX. ROSS, M.A., LL.D.,

Out of mere literary curiosity I have now and again taken the most simple word from the English Dictionary to see what could be said about it, and I have found that no word nor sentence is so insignificant, but that much sense may be found in it and much said of it. In my Magazine some years past, in exercising this curiosity I wrote a poem upon "Nothing," and which met with *eclat* from my readers, and was by many said to be worth *something*. My friends were pleased, and perhaps enlightened with "Nothing," and I was surprised at the muchness there was in *nought* and usefulness I found in *nothing at all*, for that is the meaning of Nothing. I have heard wonderful discourses from Bishops and Canons based upon a few words, and I propose in this paper to do as do they. I will take a text, and it shall be, if you please, "Beauty is but skin deep." Everybody has heard this axiom, but few have done more. A few may have said to themselves, "Yea, verily, and the Beauty may lose her *prestige* without due warning, and so precarious a thing is not worth my while to be anxious about. Very few have thought deeply upon this saying, and fewer ever commented upon it. It seems to me, who from my occupation see much beauty and great ugliness, that if it be true that beauty is but skin deep, yet such little depth of the excellence of the body is more than enough to make a great difference between one person and another. All the world is ruled by beauty. The King upon his throne, the Duke in his palace, as well as the man of letters, the man of science, the rich one, the poor one—and all are so influenced by the charms of the handsome that beauty rules our world. It is indeed mighty in attraction, and spell-binds those within a wide radius, and influences the great minds of all countries; and this is when beauty is only skin deep. The question that usually presents itself at this moment is, "What greater influence would there be where beauty is something more than so shallow as our axiom shows." Take, for instance, the excellence of contour of the head and face, which is shown in the rounding of the cheek, with its beautiful tint and its heavenly rising. The whitened forehead with its marble paleness and yet without its coolness. Surely such is more than superficial handsomeness, for both cheek and forehead is more than skin deep, whether it be produced by artificial means or otherwise; whether it has been accomplished by the use of the instrument the "Cheek Improver," or by the aid of the marble powder now so much resorted to.

It is more than "skin deep" the lustre of the human eye, the darkness that speaks with overwhelming power—a power that brings man upon his knees when the gods themselves could not do so. A power that has sent madness and despair, as well as blessing and heavenly inspiration far and wide. Can we wonder at those not gifted with this beauty applying to the organ substitutes for the natural. Can we be surprised that the toilet requisite called Eye Colour should be used to the extent it is, and when one thinks of the power of which we have just spoken, can you blame any for asking so wonderful a preparation for its aid in beauty giving. Is it a skin deep matter only when the centre feature is of Grecian shape in woman. or in the male of the aquiline outline. When the nose is of beauty's mould—of fine and short profile, smooth of surface and of septum, and nostril perfect. Compare such with the ordinary nose, and the contrast will be as great as the proboscis of the ape and the man. Yes! there are many ways of benefiting one's fellow man, and he that invents machinery or instruments for the shapening of the features or the straightening of the limbs deserves praise and reward far beyond what is given. It is much for a man to introduce means by which the foul disease small-pox shall not be rampant, and by which it shall be prevented from leaving marks or wounds over the face, but it is not so great an accomplishment for appearance as the invention of means by which a turned up, a buttoned, a hampered, awry, or a crooked nose is shaped to perfection by the painless and simple use of the "nose machine." The bold outline of a handsome chin in man, and in the dimpled and soft one of women of beauty is more than skin deep; for its form, dimple and its charm and admiration is deep in the cartilage that exists between the skin and the bone beneath, and but little in the skin itself. As an improver of personal appearance, this leads me to remark that the Chin Machine acts upon the cartilage that is beneath the flesh, and thus forms the chin to shape of proper symmetry; it acts deeper than the skin, for it leaves its mark—its impressions upon the gristle or the cushion of the skin.

The mighty man of war, the diplomist, the scientist, the learned in the arts are men evidently different to the mediocrity of the species, and so is he or she with beauty but skin deep, more contrasting than these, with the ordinary human creature. Beauty spoken of in a superficial way—only skin deep, carries all before it—every thing succumbs to it, and it behoves every one to do their best to attain such, whether it be real or only artificial.

The exquisite complexion may be skin deep only, but beauty, personal beauty, consists of more than this—symmetry of form, excellence of stature and rotundity enough, but without excess. The disadvantages of being exempt from ranking with the handsome are numerous indeed. The want of complacency, the nervous uncertainty, and the vexatious look and grimaces of those we associate with. The palpable contrast of the affability given to those with, and withheld from those without this desideratum. One's gait is improved when made handsome—one's spirits are revived and elated, and one quality acting upon another through this first grand cause enables the beauty to be happy, and to make others so, or extremely wretched, even as she pleases. It may not be considered out of place here to remark that there are very many persons closely approaching this desirable state whose personal characteristics 'are such that although nature has not made them handsome, a very little of art's work would so cause them to be. A few illustrations : how often we see a smooth skin rendered unhandsome from want of a little colour. Art can supply this nearly as well as nature herself; well shaped ears, but wrongly positioned, standing out, this can be altered by the aid of a little instrument now much used in such imperfections, and as certain in good results as the use of the " Bloom of Roses " is for diffusing of colour upon the cheek. A lustrous eye far down in the socket is ‡perfection in itself, but from its position, its excellence is lost, and is ever unappreciated until (and this is not always done) stringents are used by which the ball of vision is apparently brought forward. And so with the well formed mouth lost to view by a slight imperfection in the chin, which, until old age can be shaped.

The very hair is sometimes of that tint that borders on the beautiful, and which is carried beyond what it is by damping the hair with so trifling a thing as a little water, or a little olive oil, the one bringing out the chesnut tint, and the other intensifying the shade, so as to harmonize with the colour of the skin, either of the forehead or the neck and shoulders. Very many people are *all but* good-looking, and if they did but know how to act for their own benefit, a very little would give them the bliss of possessing a power which is greater than wealth and ranks only next to perfect health itself. The writer of these lines would be happy to receive photos of ladies and gentlemen, and advise what trivial or elaborate matter is to be carried out to alter the face and form of the decidedly ugly, or of those on the verge of beauty. Some persons are to be commended and congratulated upon being able to appreciate the excellence of handsomeness. they are alive to everything that is beautiful, and when in possession of the position where much beauty surrounds them. they are, indeed, happy, and such as these indeed may well be thought of, as being the happiest of the happy. But we must not forget that while these people are sensitive to the charms of perfection in the human form, in the picturesqueness of splendid scenery, and in all that is good in the material, they are equally sensitive to an opposite condition, and their suffering is great, when they have forced upon them the inelegant and often the ugly. The sight of premature greyness must give them a pang, and they must feel angry with the individual to whom the greyness belongs, when they recollect how easily such unnatural sights could be altered. Often before them must come the bare face of man, when innate within them is the feeling that a truly masculine face should have a beard to take off insipid and uncharacteristic looks. Ill-formed features, stiffness of stature, crooked limbs, dull complexion, obesity and attenuation must produce excessive pain in their minds which is almost maddening, and which would not surprise us if a mania ensued, displayed in utterances of the means to be employed for removing over-fatness, over leanness, excessive greyness, excessive floridness, ill-shaped-ness, and the concommitants of the inelegant and the ugly. When will the civilized world grow wiser. It is a monstrosity, or at least an anomaly, to see in our beautiful gardens, in our grand entertainments, where the very vessels we drink from are exquisite in beauty, in our architectural displays, and in our palaces, ugly men and women more often than handsome, beautifully dressed women, wearing ornaments of exquisite excellence, contrasting most strikingly with the faces and forms of the wearers. How is it that such a condition is allowed to exist? Does it come from the fact that a sentimental idea exists that it is not right, morally right, to add to or take from our bodies that which we find they possess? If it be so, it should surprise us that such an idea can exist, for its absurdity would seem most conspicuous. We are all born in ignorance, but it is the duty of our guardians to see that this is removed, that we are educated and well-informed. Our tastes are dormant, or even depressed, we are expected to cultivate good taste, and not to let ourselves remain in this as nature made us. No ; if our minds possess erroneous notions in such matters, remove them, and put in their places the correct and good thing. If ill-health is born in us, we are exhorted to take care to eat, drink, and avoid some things, and resort to others ; and yet, if we find a wart upon our noses, a palor upon our cheek, a furrow on our brow, a thin or grey head of hair, bow-legged, large hips, rotundity of form, bald heads, superfluous hair on our faces, and ill-shaped fingers and nails, we are not to bring our good taste to bear upon these subjects we are forsooth to refrain from uttering, or ondeavouring to utter. these conditions; or rather the accepted doctrine is. It is not to be known that we abhor bad personal appearances, and refrain in using means for ridding our bodies of ugliness and deformity.

THOUGHTS—MISCELLANEOUS.

By ALEX. ROSS, M.A.

How little is sufficient to make facial and bodily ugliness, and how much less to change ugliness into beauty. A pretty woman may mar her beauty by a display of anger, hate, or by grief, fatigue and illness, and so may an ugly one become attractive and bewitching by robust health, hilarity of spirits and the use of a few of the well known appliances to give tint, colour and bloom to the face, and by the aid of auxiliaries to shape the figure.

Perhaps the next in effectiveness to bad features in preventing good looks is a flabby condition of the skin of the face ; more particularly under the eyes (crow's feet) and to such a condition the handsomest of the human race are subject. Bad features previous to the introduction of the nose machine was thought irretrievable, and was endured with patient fortitude, and the loose condition was pined over mostly in middle life, but now-a-day there are fewer badly shaped features, and far less flabby, shrivelled and superfluous skin to be seen upon the face, and for which alterations we have to thank the contrivances introduced for acting by judicious pressure upon cartilagenous matter in all human faces, and to the Astringent so well known as the Skin Tonic or Skin Tightener.

It is Christmas time, and everywhere I notice comments upon books just published, with the leading statements, suited to the young, suited to the scientific, artistic and the would-be perfect men or women. It is in our natures to go with the stream; to follow others, whether it be to the good or bad, and so I find myself suggesting to those desirous of appearing personally superior to the generality of their fellows, to procure a copy of Ross's Toilet Magazine; read it carefully, and then digest its contents, that good may come to themselves and others in all matters artistic It is, I may add, sold at 1s., and may be had of any of Ross's agents, or direct from the Editor, 21, Lamb's Conduit Street, London.

———

Strange, but true—yellow and dark teeth may be made white, by using a powder suited to such a state of teeth discolouration. This powder is made of ingredients that are antidotes to the components that produce this objectionable yellowness to the teeth. We do not recommend it as a tooth powder that should always be used, for it is too powerful for such constant application. What is wanted is the removal of the coating of discolouration, and which can only be done by the use of a powerful chemical, and when such is accomplished, no further need of any powerful ingredients are necessary to keep the teeth white and pure. After such a desirable state has been obtained, an ordinary tooth powder will suffice to keep the teeth white and handsome. This may be then considered strange, but it is true.

———

Long life is not always vouchsafed to the strong, hale, and of sound constitution : for often they die early, greatly to the surprise of the sickly and long-ailing sufferer ; and so it is with the naturally handsome person, their beauty is found frequently to fail long ere it was expected so to do, whilst the mediocrity in handsomeness, or even the inelegant persons find means—artificial it may be—but still a way by which they can secure elegance, beauty and handsomeness, even to old age. The race is not always to the swift, neither is the ordinary looking person always behind the naturally handsome person, for by contriving, by studying, and by applying proper means he or she renders their person even superior to others; just as the weak and sickly one in body will, with care, contriving and discretion, manages to reach years mature, while others fall short of long life ; yea ! even leave life prematurely.

———

To some minds, strange to say, it is denied them the power of full comprehension, whilst to others, an appreciation of all things is granted ; hence a Tindal or Huxley, after their lucid description in things scientific have failed to convey their meaning to some of their audience. This state of mind is also found with regard to smaller things, and hence the want of comprehension in things of taste, in furniture, personal looks, dress and pictures. And it is this undesirable state of the mind that causes a young person not to see the enormity of premature grey hair, spareness of, and bad arrangement of this which is intended to be one of our greatest ornaments. And so with bent limbs, such a person may be knock-kneed, bow-legged, or crooked backed, but they never attempt to alter such, for their minds are callous to things of this kind—never understanding the great incongruity of a human being defaced, crippled or otherwise rendered ugly. We often come in contact with such people, and it is sorry work to expatiate, dissertate and point out imperfection which their minds are incapable of comprehending.

Restorer. This is a word that has a charm in it; one that savors of good, and is applicable to a thousand conditions, and to hundreds of things. It seems to inspire hope and cheerfulness. This association is one of the reasons for the public largely patronizing our Hair and other Restorers in the stead of a good permanent Hair Dye. There is no bewitchment in the name Dye, but much in that of Restorer, and hence the latter having perhaps a less sale than the inferior. Hair Restorers are good in their way, but from not being permanent they are inferior to Hair Dye, for with dye, the colour produced cannot be removed by any amount of rubbing or washing, and it has the advantage of being cleaner, and unattended with the disagreeable sticky feeling often complained of in liquids, such as that with so pleasing a name. I am not going to moralise, preach or prate by telling you what lesson this teaches, but I would impress upon you that though Hair Dye is not a nice name, yet it is a nice article, and much to be preferred to nearly every other article for colouring grey hair.

Analytical knowledge, obtained by chemical analysis, shows us the ingredients and quantities of such of which the blood consists, and thus we are able to trace the cause of a florid or a pale complexion. For instance, a superabundance of iron in the fluid produces redness, whilst a deficiency gives paleness, and even clearness to the skin. With power to prescribe for florid complexion, as also for pallor-clear skin, we may recommend for all imperfection in the blood the Complexion Pill, a pill for which our name has long been connected with, and which has given a world-wide satisfaction. Somebody has said, that to be good looking can be accomplished by paying attention to health and morality. This is true, to an extent, but we have seen persons, irrespective of carrying out these injunctions, handsome and pretty, and even made charming by the skill of the artist.

In an antique book, I have been reading of an industrious gentleman who rising early one morning to go to business, in his hurry and the darkness of the morn, snatched up his wife's wig, and rode ten miles before he became acquainted with the fact. He created a good deal of laughter among those he met, and from not knowing that his wife wore artificial hair, it was with difficulty he could believe he had other than his own head gear, until he looked in a glass, when—oh, gracious! he became sadly embarrassed, and hastened to return from whence he had come. How different now-a-day is hair covering; for the head is so perfectly fitted that no man could sustain upon his head that which belonged to another. *

In my profession I see much that is beautiful—made so, often by carrying out the laws of science and the genius of art. But I see more that is inelegant presented to me to remedy as best I may. Perhaps there are few greater inelegances than that of crooked legs, so often seen in young men and known to exist in the opposite sex, from the awkward gait that always follows such a condition of the lower limbs.

---

* Whips of hair are made by Alex. Ross, at 5s. up to £5, and perukes from 2 guineas to 7 guineas.

Among the many devices for pressing different parts of the body into symmetry aud excellence of position are splints, worn during the hours of sleep, and I should be glad to give the fullest particulars regarding these valuable instruments to comfort and elegance.

The imperfections of our bodies are sometimes as accidental as our names—ill shaped head, bent limbs, receding eyes and high cheeks we inherit as much as we do our names. But these bodily distresses are unlike our cognomen, in as much as the imperfections of our bodies we may alter by artifice, but our names are always the same (providing we are males).

To be agile, flexible and graceful in movement, is indicative of health and youthfulness; and this condition, more or less, may be assumed by the somewhat advanced in life in dispersing superfluity of obeseness— creating elegance of features, hilarity of spirits, and symmetrical limbs, the latter produced by correct direction of out-growing joints and out-standing bones.

Many good things become bad from taking them, using them, and re-sorting to them too much. This is applicable to eating, drinking, and dressing. The use of toilet artifices, contrivances, inventions and dis-coveries is good for all to avail themselves of; and it is only when the use of dyes, paints, enamels and skin astringents are applied in excess of time and means that anything in truth can be said against them.

Permit me to preach, by saying, Doing to others as we would have them do to us, is exemplified by a man giving attention to his appear-ance, as does his wife and friends around him: he thus reciprocates the good he obtains from the tasty appearance of his closest companions.

Small Pox marks are very painful to look at, very distressing to the ones marred by them, who would often give half they possess to know how to hide them from the gaze of their fellows. Well! this is ac-complished by using a pigment of suitable consistency, which is smeared into the marks with the thumb and finger. A fact well deserving a *mem* in your diary, that you may assist those despairing of ever hiding these eyesores.

I have just seen a letter written in vindication of a proper amount of attention being given to the study of personal appearance, and among the many things said were these. Woman is known to be the most beautiful of creation, and therefore it behoves her to amend any imper-fection in her appearance that time or illness may cause. She is the superior in excellence of beauty and delight, and knowing her mission, her status in the world, she is aware that every imperfection, or the lessening of any charm, should have her prompt and speedy attention, for she being the sweet companion of man, she has the conscientious impulse that the longer she remains such, the better for herself and for her friends. Hence the justification of using every means to enhance beauty, and every suitable invention to amend facial and symmetrical imperfections.

Why does hair fall after an illness?   Why does greyness present itself speedily and in plenty subsequent to grief and anxiety?   There are many explanations of this given in books pathological, but the opinion of one devoted to the study of this particular is that the root of the hair is loosely set in the lowest strata of the skin, and is in close proximity of the blood from which it draws its colour and its life itself.   Passing through the cuticle, it penetrates the epidermis, and is kept in position and tightly held by the pores of the skin.   When these pores relax from illness, the hair is easily drawn out, hence the loss of hair after sickness through the pores loose and relaxed condition.   Then, as to greyness.   It is engendered by a deficiency of iron in the blood, for as the ingredient iron is the reason of the fluid being red, so also is it the sole source from which hair obtains its shade; lessen the quantity of iron in the system, and then you not only lose colour in the face, but in the hair, whether it be whisker or hair on the head.

A great deal of poetry has been written upon the foot, even more than upon the hand, and we are not surprised that it is so, for there is a charm in a perfectly shaped foot, attractive to all who have seen it.   Only treat the foot with the same consideration as you give to the hand, and an improvement will follow that will add fresh pleasure when you contemplate upon your reflection in the glass that depicts you from head to foot. If you ask what I mean by attention to the feet equal to that of the hands, I would say use the little instrument introduced by myself for shapening the toe nails, a contrivance that after their horney substance is softened, presses them into good shape, and that by merely wearing these during a few nights without inconvenience or even knowledge of their presence.

Then I would suggest that the enlarged toe joint be treated, so that it looks less ugly, less red and burning, stiff and tender; its inflammation may be subdued, and the foreign substance, or matter, semi-substance may be dispersed by using suitable means; the secret of which I should be glad to give to those so inconvenienced as to have a big toe equal to two healthy ones.   Render your feet elegant, divested of all abnormal condition, and you will have symmetry in shape, agility of movement, graceful step and alacrity, with a perfect balance of the body that will give you a power and a charm which the half cripple will never possess :

> "How her feet tempt; how soft and light she treads,
> Fearing to wake the flowers from their beds.
> Yet, from their sweet green pillows everywhere
> They start, and gaze about to see my fair."

Herrick the poet wrote—

> "——— Her pretty feet
> Like snails did creep
> A little out, and then—
> As if they started at bo-peep
> Did soon draw in again."

The great disfigurer of the feet—the hard excrescences termed corns, should be treated to a dose of the liquid commented upon in an advertisement found in another page.

It is a wise provision, that the inhabitants of countries in the

Torrid Zone are supplied with more hair than the African, Bedouin, and others living in warm climates. Massive beards and thick heads of hair are the heritage of the Scotch, whilst the Egyptians have smooth faces and short crisp hair on their heads.

Hair is variously treated and variously fashioned. In Germany the men all ape the military, and it is the desire of all in that country to remove the hair from the sides of the face and increase it upon the upper lip. A clean shaved face, save and except the upper lip, is considered military in appearance, and is aimed at by all men both young and old. Now, as the worthies age, a certain indication of such is apparent from the old look of the stubble of the hair on the sides of the face; at sixty, these sides that have been shorn for perhaps forty years, have a very dark and dirty appearance, and at seventy the skin becomes flabby, which in connection with the dirty appearance—causes the owners to resort to some process for destroying the root of the hair *within* the skin. In such cases as these an ordinary "Depilatory" will be of but little service, so they resort to stronger measures. The process is kept rather secret, and perhaps I am not acting worldly wisely in writing it out here; but knowing as I do that there are very many of both sexes greatly annoyed in having upon their faces surperfluous hair, I give this information that they may be encouraged in the hope that yet they may be able to reduce that objectionable dark shade cast upon their countenances by the root of hair shown through the skin, which not only clouds their faces materially, but does also mentally.

The process is something like this—Water—warm impregnated with a softening compound, is first used in bathing the face, or that part of it where hair is growing or has grown. When the skin has been well dried, a geletinous preparation of an emollient character is rubbed vigorously into the flesh, and is repeated several times. Then a paste of a peculiar character is rubbed into the skin with the points of the fingers, and having done its work, which it will have done in fifteen or twenty minutes, the face is again washed with the chemically prepared warm water. After this, the skin is found to be in a beautiful soft condition, and all seems to be as anyone could desire. In order to keep up this clear condition of the skin, daily for a short time, a manipulating with a curious preparation is necessary, and this having been done all is supposed to be finished, and to end to the satisfaction of the operator and the operated upon. As may be seen, the use of the means requires no skill, and one can apply the means themselves, providing they have the ingredients, and I may here intimate that I should be happy to give the fullest information upon the subject, and supply the preparations necessary.

What a diversity of faces we see; what different expressions they have; let this induce each of my readers to look in the glass and observe the expression of their own faces, and if such expression is not desirable, let them alter it. Love is expressed by a fair, clear and pleasant countenance. An old writer says such should have no clouds, wrinkles or unpleasant tendings; the forehead should have an ample height and breadth, with majestic grace, and a full eye with a fine shadow at the bottom of the eyelid and a little at the corner. The nose should be proportionable, a clear cheek, a smiling mouth—the mouth line should be shadowed at the corners.

Any artistic persons can produce these effects more or less upon their countenances; and there are some desirous for these pleasing traces to be on their faces and unacquainted with the art of producing them. Let them apply to the writer of these few words, who will readily advise.

The expression of fear is unmistakeable; the eyes fall back, they look heavy, and downwards; the thin cheeks—the mouth close—with the hair careless in arrangement. Surely any person after reading the instructions given in this small pamphlet, might alter such a condition where needed.

Persons meeting with accidents, receiving bruises in the face, are in the habit of applying to me to paint these black and blue discolourations from the soft and pink flesh shade. This I do, and for a time the bruises are coverered, and he or she is thus enabled to present themselves in society. They can be repainted when necessary until nature rids them of the effects of the accident by its healing powers. Why is this not done in cases where the skin is discoloured by birth marks and old wounds if a more permanent remedy be not applied as recommended elsewhere.

Persons necessitated to appear in public, whether they be ill or well, whether their faces are pallid from headache, or yellow and black under the eyes from biliousness, endure greatly from their knowledge of the fact that they are not pleasing in appearance; they endure a double agony from the feeling that they are not only not looking their best, but are positively looking their worst. A lady at a party, where her friends have assembled, having done their utmost to make themselves refined and elegant in appearance, or the much admired singer at the concert, or the prima donna on the stage, suffer mentally far more than headache or biliousness in the feeling that every one is looking at the sallow complexion, the bilious eye, and the blackened crows feet under that organ.

It is true some are wiser than others, and cover over more or less these imperfections, but these are the few, and we beg to put it forth as a boon to persons positioned as we have just said that they learn the art of using suitable articles to cover over the blackened eye, yellow skin, and jaundiced looking features. Information would be gladly given by me to the use of any means for increasing good looks and lessening ill ones, and so adding enjoyment and happiness where otherwise would be misery and even agony.

If you want to look tall, wear (I am speaking to the ladies) clothing that is not stiff and rigid, but flowing garments; let the pattern, if any, be more or less of perpendicular lines; let the hair be dressed high, and not brought over the face more than possible. Let it be borne in mind that when persons look downwards—when they look upon the earth rather than upon the sky, they look an inch or two shorter than when they throw the face upwards and thus raise the whole of the body, giving it elegance and grace.

"You seem to have a remedy for every imperfection," said one who had profited by the use of contrivances for improving the appearance of those physically imperfect. Our answer might have been, No; we have no means by which we currently make a badly shaped head perfect. But this we can do make apparently the cranium of good form by suggesting in the male how the hair should be lessened here and thickened there; how to wear the hair, and where to flatten it, as also where best to raise it from the scalp, where to have the parting, and where to make no parting at all.

To the opposite sex, we would suggest how to arrange the feathers and other ornaments worn. The contour to the head may be greatly altered for the better by an examination of it by the aid of a hand glass in front of a larger mirror, and by pressing, where wanted, and raising where necessary to correct outline.

Any pleasant evening when the weather is congenial, it is a pleasant sight to see the ladies leaving their carriages and passing into the concert rooms and theatres of our great London. All is, however, changed if the weather be bad and an easterly wind be blowing. Instead of the uniform complexion seen in congenial weather, there is an irregularity of colour. The eyes and nose are red—even bordering upon the blue— whilst the cheeks are pale, and the forehead rough in look. Unfortunately it is only a few that are acquainted with the means for altering this— for preventing the redness and coarse look which the countenance has when a dry, cold wind is blowing, which sadly affects both the skin and the temper.

SHAPENING THE FINGERS AND NAILS.

By ALEX. ROSS, M.A.

THE fingers of the human hand are of great importance in good appearance. Those well shaped denote good caste, and those of superior shape are taken as being of undisputed aristocracy. Manual labour spoils the appearance of the fingers, as they become shaped to the convenience of the work upon which they are engaged. There is no disgrace in having bent fingers, but it is a sign of belonging to the working class, whilst the well-formed ones indicate just the opposite, and my lord and my lady never have a hand the same as the persons in lower grade than they. It is a well known fact, that we all imitate the higher class; and it is well we do so, when the example before us is tasty, superior, and good. No person need have a hand other than of good conditions, however much such may be used in manual labour, providing he or she will carry out tested plans for their preservation and for their proper shape. With a hand that is hardly worked, it is stretched—its fingers are spread, flattened, and ill-shaped; whilst the nails become short, bruised, and flat. In cases of sudden death, of found bodies, and descriptions of persons discovered under suspicious circumstances, the hands are the first part of the examination, and they are recognized as belonging to the upper, middle, or lower class. This striking difference of shape and form may be altered by using a trough or cradle, as it is called, made in such a way that the finger or thumb may be laid in it, and when not quite of proper size its composition is such that it may be shaped as required, so as to perfectly accommodate the finger it contains. This cradle, or trough, after the finger is laid in it, is surrounded with broad ribbon, making a compress that shapes the nails as well as the points of the fingers. The patient arranges these contrivances night after night for a short time, and is rewarded by fingers of exquisite symmetry and nails rivalling the filbert nut in shape. Any one proposing to themselves the wearing of these shapeners of the fingers, should before applying them lay their hands upon a clean sheet of paper and pass a lead pencil round them, thus leaving a perfect representation on the paper of what their hand is at the present moment, and by dong the same thing after using the contrivance for a week or two ; they would be greatly surprised at the pleasing alteration made in so short a time. The action upon the nails may be facilitated by plentifully supplying them 'with warm water, by which they are made malleable, so that the compress easily shapes them. Many persons may think it of little importance as to what appearance the hand has, but when we recollect how pleasant a sight it is to see a hand outstretched of colour and shape exquisite—it is surely worth our time and study to obtain a fac-simile of such. I have only just finished an interview with a black doctor, one who has studied in this country and obtained methodical learning and practice, and upon showing him my many devices, the principle of which is pressure, he was fully convinced of the success that must follow their use. The explanations I gave him were as lucid and clear as I was master of, and he was agreeably sur prised; but when he asked me for my greatest wonder—my largest accomplishment—I think I more than astonished him when I stated that I had a liquid that would remove the colour from moles, no matter how deep a shade, and that being able to do this with moles, I could remove the black from the skin of a coloured man. With all politeness I argued the matter, and he left me, I believe, a wiser man, complimenting me upon this achievement as well as that of shapening by pressure. Well, then, I think I have nothing more to say upon the good shape of the nails and fingers being easily obtained. More than this, that no lady or gentleman should allow their hands to be disfigured when by little expense and little trouble perfectly formed ones may be had. These contrivances are sold at 3s. 6d. the pair. Many persons use a pair only at the time, putting them upon the fingers at night, removing them in the morning. So much for the fingers. The hand is treated with a compress only, and is treated independently of the fingers ; this hardens the flesh where necessary, and softens it where desirable, at the same time whitens and removes marks and unevenness.

THE SKIN TIGHTENER.

By ALEX. ROSS, M.A.

Some years ago, when I first made the discovery that the pores of the skin could be readily acted upon, and the muscles facial could be brought from an abnormal to a natural condition, I was met with incredulous looks and speech certainly not implying belief. But great has been the change since then, for now the supply of a liquid invented at that time is asked for over and over again, and is used by thousands to tighten the tissue of the skin and the muscles of the face. When by observation and deductions drawn from facts in connection with the relaxed condition of the skin of the face, I produced a preparation of an astringent character, it explained to all interested that such a thing was practicable, and they exclaimed either by gesture or vocally, "Yea, verily! what a wonder such was never thought of before." Most medical men, when they first heard of the significant name "Skin Tightener," looked dubiously; but when from analysis it was found that an astringent was the basis of its character, all expression of unbelief vanished, and they allowed that an astringent was the only thing that possibly could render service in tightening the skin. Of course, it is one thing to know upon what principle a matter is accomplished, and another to carry properly and fully out the principle involved; and so has it been with all those who have endeavoured to imitate this excellent preparation for removing furrows and indentations in the skin. Many a young person at eighteen years of age find a dark mark proceeding from just under the eye and extending for an inch downwards, which, as years go on, curves, and forms the *crow's foot* so much dreaded by those who would keep their good appearance and would not age in look rapidly. It is not always that the healthiest escape these marks in the early part of their womanhood, for we note that it is often the case that the delicate have an even skin, whilst the buxom and strong possess these signs of age and preliminary of fading beauty. Furrows, however, seldom make their appearance in the faces of the young; and care, illness, and vexation, bring them with a certainty after the age of thirty. The "Skin Tightener" of course has a limit as to its efficacy—miracles it cannot work, and if you apply it to faces bereft of teeth, health and are attenuated, it may fail, probably, in making such what they were before. But for all that, much will be accomplished, and if the owner would have artificial teeth, feed and medicine the body as it should be, the Skin Tightener would do the rest. With medicine, a proper and stated quantity is prescribed, and if more than this portion be taken, evil is done in the stead of the good. Not so with the Skin Tightener, the more there is used, the better and more speedy the result—too much cannot be used; indeed the quantity applied regulates the good done. The face, people are tenacious about, and most ladies who are not acquainted with this useful preparation, ask me, " Will it do any harm ; can it be used improperly, so as to injure the skin; is there any other results, that may make the flesh worse than before?" Certainly not; it is in every way a good preparation, and I would have my patients mark that not only is the Tonic a harmless article, but it is more, for it is a remedial liquid, and will cure and benefit the skin in every case of imperfection. An infant a week old might be bathed in it and it would prove to be beneficial. If another proof be wanted of the good done by this now highly valued astringent, I would say that in using it to the skin, much good is found from pouring it into the sockets of the eyes and then raising the lids, letting the liquid come in contact with the pupils, keeping the eye well open, and thus giving comfort to the orb, lustre to its iris, and whiteness to its surrounding. Then its application is not intricate, it is most simple, and only one thing to be kept in remembrance is, it must be used plentifully —even prodigally. The best plan to adopt, perhaps, is this. Let the face be perfectly clean and quite dry, and free from perspiration. Let a small white handkerchief be well wetted with the Tonic or Skin Tightener, and let it be placed over the whole of the upper part of the face, reaching downwards to the point of the nose, now pressing the handkerchief well into the sockets of the eyes, and pass the hand over those parts of the handkerchief that cover the loose part of the face and the flabby flesh often found near the nostrils; let the furrows be pressed so as to receive their full share of the means for their removal. This all being properly attended to, the user may now let the Tonic dry into the face, and if it has been applied after retiring to rest, then the eyes may be closed and sleep invited. The lower part of the face may be treated in the same way, whilst some persons cover the whole of the face at one time; the only inconvenience being that when the nose and mouth are both covered at the same time, the covering cannot be placed so close to the skin as is desirable. I may say that several applications are required in some cases, whilst with others a very few usings will suffice, and one thorough applying is enough to make a noticeable difference in every face so favoured.

The loose flesh of the hand is remedied by well wetting a lisle thread glove with the Tonic and wearing the same for an hour or two during the day, or kept upon the hand during the hours of sleep.

Should these few lines upon an important subject—for important it is —be read by ladies abroad, they are invited to have the " Tonic or Skin Tightener " sent out to them in a granulated form, so that it can be sent as an ordinary letter, costing very little more for postage than would ordinary correspondence. It is pleasing to find difficult cases of long standing have submitted to the treatment I have been suggesting by my receiving communications from abroad and at home, with expressions of gratitude for good accomplished. These written commendations I should be happy to show, as far as I am permitted so to do, by the sender, to those ladies who are desirous to know of persons having found full benefit from the Skin Tightener.

HATS, PAST AND PRESENT.

SOME little time back a good deal appeared in the scientific and other papers regarding Heads and Hats. From the assertion made by an old established hatter, that the circumference of the interior of the head covering had greatly lessened during the last 30 years, caused the thinker and investigator of cause and effect to draw the conclusion that heads were diminishing in size, and as a matter of course inferred that small heads were reduced in quantity of intellectual power. This conclusion was conducive to a great deal of controversy among lovers of their kind, and those anxious for the march of intellect. It was no argument that the present generation was more civilized than its predecessor, as the latter had accomplished as much in paving the way for the former as had led to our present high state of intellectual power. And as the clique who persisted that the degeneracy of our race was undergoing an undesirable change, a few scientific men buckled to, to assign reasons for this *apparent* discrepancy—that of heads capable of wearing small hats being of no less size than those who had worn larger. By the measuring of skulls now and again obtained of those long ago put to rest, could, one would have thought, settled the question. The circumference of the head of skulls the writer had in his possession, with the measurement taken, it may be, in at least a hundred other collections, would prove, we think, to most minds that in the average heads of both male and female, remained about the same in circumference as they had been for the last century. The contention has risen, not upon any very great variation in sizes of heads, for the asserters merely contend for three-eights of an inch in circumference, so that there requires a very nice calculation in placing the tape round the craniums of both living and dead heads ; you have to allow for the long or short or thick hair of one or both, for the rich full skin, within its semi-cartilaguous matter between the skin and bone in the living, and for its deficiency more or less in the dead.

Well, this is one way of settling the question. Another is by pointing out the fact the measurement for hats is now less in size, from the hair being worn cut close to the head, indeed so close that 30 years ago had men so worn their hair they would have been pointed out as having been in prison, or had just returned from penal servitude. Now, in days of which it is said it was necessary for hats to be larger than they now are, the powder and paste upon long curling or plaited hair would make a considerable difference, even more, we think, than the three-eights of an inch. In the days of William IV. and later on, the fashion for mediocrity was to wear caps, whilst the men engaged in mental pursuits, the clergy, and professional men wore hats ; and it is fair to assume that as larger heads are possessed by those capable of mental work, that the special hats—those only for big heads—should not be compared with those worn by every class, as in the days in which we live.

Added to this, fashion not only varies what is worn, and of what shape and form, but how adjusted, how placed upon its devotee. Our grandfathers thought it the right way of wearing the hat far in the nape of the neck, and even over the ears, whilst we wearers of hats place them more upon the top of the head, and thus being away from the base, and nearing the apex lessens the size of what we now cover our heads with. I may add, that there is almost as much diversity in size of a man's hat as there is in a lady's bonnet; and we can all recollect the contrast in our grandmother's, and our sister's, or lady friends bonnets.

The established hatter of which we have spoken seems to have had a very select connection, for he mentions the dimensions of the hats of the leading men of thirty years past, and contrasts them with those of to-day, but no anthropologicalist would believe in the degeneracy of intellect from such an imperfect argument in the opposite direction, for even the examination of a few pictures of aged date will shew us illustrations of the larger hats worn by our progenitors, and from which the deduction may be drawn that our sires were deficient in good taste or artistic qualities, and that we were less disposed to inartistic dress, and that our heads were no smaller nor our brains of lesser quantity nor quality.

In making the above remarks, I would intimate that many men render themselves somewhat disfigured by the head gear they wear; and although they are aware that they have chosen cap or hat unsuitable to their appearance, they are at a loss to know how best to act. They would be thankful for reliable information as to what best suits their height, complexion, breadth and features. But they know none whose profession is that of studying harmony, contrast, and detraction connected with dress, and therefore I would apprise them of the fact that I have been engaged in this assistance to the well-dressed public for many years past, and should be happy to extend my practice.—ALEX. ROSS, M.A., 21, Lamb's Conduit Street, London, W. C., near the Foundling.

A FEW TESTIMONIALS FROM PERSONS
WHO HAVE TESTED THE ARTICLES MENTIONED.

I obtained the "Nose Machine," and am very much pleased with it.

Thanks to your Machine my nose has attained a tolerably symmetrical shape.

Please to send me a larger bottle of the Tonic, (Skin Tightener), as I find a benefit from it.

Having seen already the wonderful effects of your Cosmetiques, I would be greatly obliged if you would send me, &c.

Will you kindly send me one of your Nose Machines. A friend of mine having used one with great success.

The above are quotations from letters received by me, and may tend to establish facts more, from coming from clients, than from anything I may say. I have put them here as much to fill up this Pamphlet as for the proof they may give of the assertions made herein; and doubtless I should never have put them in print, had not the printer intimated that he wanted a little more copy. More letters of commendation I could have quoted from, were it required, but I refrain, as very many may be seen in my numerous other printed matter.

Celebrated Inventions, &c.

PREPARED AND SOLD BY

ALEX. ROSS, M.A., LL.D.

EAR MACHINE.—This instrument has the characteristic, that it gives the exact amount of Pressure required to making the ears properly positioned. Price 10s. 6d., sent for 6d. extra, secretly packed.

ENLARGED TOE JOINTS.—By the use of a compress well saturated with a liquid known as Ross' Preparation for Enlarged Joints, great relief and goodness of shape is obtained. 3s. 6d. per bottle.

FINGER SHAPERS.—These are small instruments in which the points of the fingers are laid, and then pressed into good shape, by which the nails and the points of the fingers are quickly beautified. 3s. 6d.

OVER-STOUTNESS is dispersed by carrying out regulations as given by Alex. Ross. A certain alteration for the better is made in 14 days, as may be tested by weighing from time to time. Fee 5s.

MAGNETO ELECTRIC MACHINE.—May be used with the greatest success for stopping the hair from falling, and for increasing its growth. Price 21s.

HIP BANDS.—For forming the Hips that are squatty and inelegant into good shape. Price 21s.

SPLINTS FOR BOW LEGS, IN-GROWING KNEES, and for **FEET** and **LIMBS** not quite straight and well-portioned. 10s. 6d. and 21s.

FLORID COMPLEXION toned down by using astringent liquids to the skin. 3s. 6d. per bottle.

KNEE CAPS, for pressing in the knees, and thus lengthening the limbs, giving height, commonly called tallness.

TATTOO MARKS, and all marks removed from the skin, by using a Bleaching Liquid, which is quite harmless. It takes the colour from Moles, &c. Price 3s. 6d.

ARTIFICIAL NOSES.—Persons not able to visit Mr. Ross on account of distance, can have them made to perfection, by sending Photo, and a few particulars as to complexion and age. Price two guineas.

A SIMPLE CONTRIVANCE FOR IMPROVING THE FIGURE by drawing back the shoulders, and Expanding the Chest, price 7s. 6d., by post. 7s. 9d.

EYE COLOUR is a preparation for Dressing the Eye. It consists of three Preparations, one for the eyebrows and lash, another for giving seeming size to the organ, and one for hiding any marks around it. The second preparation is of a peculiar blue character, which is put amongst the hair of the lower lash, producing a wonderful effect, 3s. 6d. or 6d. stamps.